DILEMMAS IN CRIMINOLOGY

McGRAW-HILL SOCIAL PROBLEMS SERIES

Marvin B. Sussman, Series Editor

The purpose of this series is to provide new and improved materials for teaching the introductory course in social problems. In order to serve the needs of this and related courses the series brings together a set of stimulating and thought-provoking original volumes which deal with the traditional social problem areas. By covering relevant theory and research, each volume becomes a provocative study of ideas and conceptualizations rather than a descriptive account of a particular social problem. Each provides a theoretical framework relative to the problem under study. Together the volumes offer the instructor an opportunity to develop an integrative conceptual framework for the introductory social problems course.

NOW AVAILABLE

J. Milton Yinger •	A MINORITY GROUP IN AMERICAN SOCIETY
Harrison M. Trice •	ALCOHOLISM IN AMERICA
Leonard Savitz •	DILEMMAS IN CRIMINOLOGY

IN PREPARATION

Samuel Bloom •	MENTAL HEALTH
Marvin B. Sussman •	FAMILY
Robert Dentler •	COMMUNITY
Vincent H. Whitney •	POPULATION
William A. Faunce •	PROBLEMS OF AN INDUSTRIAL SOCIETY

DILEMMAS IN CRIMINOLOGY

LEONARD SAVITZ
Associate Professor of Sociology

Temple University

McGRAW-HILL BOOK COMPANY
New York · St. Louis · San Francisco · Toronto · London · Sydney

The book *Dilemmas in Criminology* is a unique one. As the title indicates, it does not present an overall treatment of criminology but rather discusses in depth some of the basic dilemmas inherent in the field and the problems faced by individuals trying to make sense of the causes, processes, treatment, and outcomes of antisocial behavior. Before we proceed further, it is important to examine what a dilemma is.

In logic, "dilemma" refers to an argument in which an opponent is faced with two alternatives, both of which will be conclusive against him. By extension, it can refer to any situation in which the possibilities of action or argument are equally unattractive; and by a very loose extension it is sometimes used to refer to any particularly difficult problem. Professor Savitz is using the more precise definition and applying it to situations involving choice among possible courses of action. According to Professor Savitz, dilemmas are "situations which require choosing a course of action from among several unsatisfactory alternatives, none of which is demonstrably superior to any of the others."

Professor Savitz presents a number of problems which involve equally unsatisfactory alternatives. Some involve conflicting contemporary practices, orientations, or values, and for these Professor Savitz describes the alternative decisions that could be made and the limitations of each.

In the field of criminology there are varying definitions of terms such as "crime," "criminal," "deviant behavior," and "delinquency." The use of such terms varies according to the definitions given by particular individuals. Conceptualizing an act as a crime is a relative rather than an absolute phenomenon. An act called a crime in one region may not be considered such in another. Since these definitions vary, is not the elimination of delinquent behavior or crime impossible? If definitions are transient and relative, it means that we will always have some behavior called delinquent or criminal.

An important question which Professor Savitz raises is whether there is in our society a greater concern with criminals, especially those individuals who act violently and abuse others, than with crime itself. Related to this question is another contradiction. We are deeply concerned about violence and being protected from violence, but we nevertheless ignore those who act violently if they do not involve us. A classic example is that of Kitty Genovese, who was stabbed to death in the streets of New York while observers and passersby did not heed her cries. When asked why they did not intervene, they answered, "It was none of our business." The varying definitions of crime; whether we should focus on the elimination of crime or just the containment of the violent criminal; whether we rectify wrong when we see it—these are major problems in criminology.

Data on crime and delinquency such as those collected by the Federal Bureau of Investigation and the Federal Bureau of Prisons and reported in the *Uniform Crime Reports* are used to support the formulation of policies and programs to curb criminal and delinquent behavior. At best such collections of data are less than complete or accurate. This is because of variations in reporting by local jurisdictions and differences in defining and reporting criminal and delinquent acts in various parts of the society. The extent and degree of enforcement of statutes among different jurisdictions is another variable affecting the reliability of the reported data. But although these deficiencies exist, we find that public officials, students of criminology, and others—some with an ax to grind—use the data to support their personal biases concerning what are appropriate and legitimate criminological practices. Data of questionable accuracy are used as authoritative sources and become the bases for policy changes, creation of new institutions, and the development of reform movements in many parts of the country.

In our society, existing and new social control institutions develop policies and practices in order to handle deviants. Most of the policies and practices are based on an evaluation of accumulated experience and on judgments, often biased, derived from a set of preordained values. A problem arises when research efforts provide evidence which indicates that changes are needed in policies, programs, and institutional arrangements. Will changes occur as a consequence of significant research findings? For example, Professor Savitz discusses a study in which the possibility is raised that a neighborhood undergoing class, ethnic, or racial transition and reaching a "tip-point," when it becomes more homogeneous, may display a downward incidence of delinquency and criminal behavior as homogeneity increases. Suppose it was discovered that this reduction in delinquency was a result of self-policing practices of the class, ethnic, or racial group becoming predominant. Would local law enforcement change its policies to take advantage of this, or would it retain the old rigid policies? In order for the findings of research to be followed up in this way, they would have to be as nearly unquestionable as possible. And this requires that research be carried out scientifically. Professor Savitz is concerned with the way criminologists are caught between public demands for immediate results and their own knowledge that they cannot produce better results until they have a great deal more data from research. The dilemma involved here is that doing research scientifically enough to make it truly useful entails some unattractive choices.

Tested or untested theories of criminology which are communicated, articulated, and commonly accepted may demand basic, long-range changes in the patterns of institutional life in the society. For instance, changes in the allocation of resources might remove many of the economic bases for deviant behavior. The primary question is whether such basic changes should be introduced for a possible payoff which is a long way off or whether monies, time, and energy should be spent on short-range programs which may have immediate remedial effects. A program providing counseling, social work, and job information services for potential delinquents, for example, may aid specific individuals in avoiding criminal careers, but it does not remove the economic deprivation that characterizes much of the life of the lower classes in society. This brings up a basic dilemma dealt with by Professor Savitz. The dilemma in essence is whether criminological theories should be true or practical. That is, should a theory be a true and complete model of explanation, or should it lead immediately to a workable program? There are two reasons why both may not be possible. First, there is the problem of limited time and limited resources. Second, a true theory may have no really practical implications, or it may imply enormous social changes which are not feasible.

In all societies law-enforcement agencies are given authority and power, and the use of force is legitimatized in order to provide for the protection of the citizen against encroachments by deviants. This is a large and serious responsibility; yet, as Professor Savitz points out, most law-enforcement agencies are held in low repute by a suspicious and sometimes hostile public. Associated with this position of low esteem is the belief that the police are basically corrupt, inefficient, and oftentimes brutal and that their ranks are filled by individuals rejected from employment in other occupations. This is a problem of major significance confronting law-enforcement agencies and the public today. The dilemma in the area of law enforcement centers on the fact that if more power is given to those who enforce the law the citizenry is left with fewer civil rights. The major task is to adjust the granting of power to maintain the civil rights of both the public and the accused individual. An illustration of this dilemma is the current confusion and conflict over the creation of private review boards to evaluate police practices. Each police system requires that it control its own members. Furthermore, the maintenance of its organization depends upon the power and authority of those in control. Such power and authority over the members of the police system are needed in order to maintain discipline and a system of reward and punishment. Yet such autonomous systems can abuse others in their use of power, especially in dealing with outsiders. The question is whether the abuses can be reduced by having a lay board review police practices. This is a problem of major proportion: How can we preserve the autonomous law-enforcement system and at the same time ensure that the system will not commit abuses in the performance of its functions?

The varied procedures of criminal justice—the police powers of arrest, interrogation, extracting the confession, wiretapping, and booking the suspect; trial by a judge or a jury; and many other processes—are meant to protect the general population. A dilemma results from the relationship of these acts to due process of law, protection of civil rights, equal treatment before the law, privacy of the home, etc. Is it possible to engage in a variety of acts that can end by virtually stripping the individual of his rights and privileges as a free human being and still protect his rights and those of others? This is another of the dilemmas in criminology.

Professor Savitz has devoted a major section in this volume to the dilemma involved in the punishment of criminals. Professor Savitz discusses three possible objectives for punishment: revenge, incapacitation, and rehabilitation. These are mutually exclusive, he holds, and none is provably better than the others. A possible analysis of the problem is that we in fact punish for "social revenge" but in theory are dedicated to the ideal of rehabilitation. Other institutions for the deviant are basically total and monolithic ones with their own social systems, norms, and values. They strip the individual of his freedom, of his privacy, and oftentimes of his identity. They create a new identity for the incarcerated individual which perpetuates itself even after release from prison. How do these practices fit in with the modern concept of rehabilitation—the idea that persons who commit deviant acts should be given a chance to redeem themselves through a program including vocational, social, and psychological rehabilitation? It seems illogical to expect that typical prisoners will be prepared to resume creative and contributory places in society and that they will be accepted and welcomed in the community as citizens forgiven for their previous errors.

Professor Savitz also discusses serious questions related to our concept of rehabilitation and the insistence upon capital punishment for major crimes in many of our jurisdictions.

A student will find that in the presentation of the numerous dilemmas in criminology in this book he is forced to think of the reasons for these predicaments and invited to explore the topics further in the references cited by the author. In a sense, this book raises more questions than it answers. It reveals that it is difficult to understand the phenomenon of criminal behavior and its control—let alone to solve the dilemmas within it. The student will note that Professor Savitz has touched upon important issues, some so sensitive that many students of criminology avoid discussing them or ignore their treatment. The student should investigate each dilemma carefully and see if he can come up with a resolution. Professor Savitz suggests possible solutions to these dilemmas, and these possibilities should be evaluated. One conclusion to be drawn from this book is that there are real dilemmas and that we have to live with them. Our task is to juggle apparently contradictory solutions, to evaluate the conditions and times in relation to each suggested solution, and then to choose a single alternative as the best one. Perhaps at a later time and under different circumstances another alternative may be more appropriate. It appears that deviant behavior in all its dimensions and manifestations, from how it is controlled to how it is perceived, requires adoption of the notion of a dilemma and acceptance of an alternative which is often less than satisfactory.

Marvin B. Sussman

CONTENTS

DILEMMAS IN CRIMINOLOGY

INTRODUCTION

Many Americans today surely feel that contemporary America, even more than eighteenth-century Europe, deserves to be considered an Age of Reason. Rationality, science, and enlightenment prevail and will shortly provide cures, if they have not already done so, for problems which have plagued mankind since its beginnings. We seem to have reached a point when science will soon produce "magical keys" to unlock universal secrets and make more understandable and controllable those social pathologies which are, increasingly, a sign of our times. No longer do we take a family outing to Bedlam to visit and bedevil the insane for our amusement and sport. Mental illness is finally recognized as a psychological disease, not very different from other illnesses, for which research will someday produce complete cures. Homosexuality, so recently considered despicable and filthy is no longer universally regarded as a sin and, if recent experiences in England and Illinois correctly reflect current attitudes, may be classified less and less as criminal or even symptomatic of emotional disturbances. It will perhaps come to be thought of as a permissible form of sexual behavior between consenting adults.

We are even coming to view drug addiction, once considered the ultimate depravity, as a sickness requiring medical and psychiatric treatment, not condemnation and punishment. Certainly there has been similar acceptance, however superficial, of the same rationalistic approach to the amorphous area of behavior called crime and delinquency. At the present time it is difficult to adhere to a genetic or biological explanation of criminal behavior or to believe that the criminal is a product of a set of immutable factors.

But the point of this discussion is that this general agreement on the modifiability of criminogenic elements represents only the slightest nod in the direction of science and research. We can all agree that crime is bad; that the causal factors will, in time, be explicable; and that science, even the cruder variety practiced in the social sciences, will yield sufficient insight to permit the creation of effective programs for preventing social deviance or at least holding it to an irreducible minimum. We cannot, however, jump from these pleasant reflections to the belief that the problem is virtually solved. It simply is not possible at the present time to set up a series of workable programs which would effectively curb delinquency. After affirming that science is wonderful, we cannot then conclude that we may bid delinquency farewell if we spend sufficient money to put enough workers into the field to "deal" with the delinquent and to initiate enough action programs. The trouble is that there persists an almost universal assumption that sufficient knowledge of the causes of crime is in fact available and known to all but the most backward criminologists. The mass media, policy makers in government, *soi-disant* experts on the American scene— all reinforce the notion that juvenile delinquency stems from poverty, broken homes, school dropouts, segregation, and discrimination. Despite all this, the fact is that such facile answers do not currently exist; it might therefore prove profitable to analyze in detail several basic concepts, data, research, and theory in the field of criminology. It is necessary, however, to indicate several of the dilemmas that inevitably arise in any discussion of crime—situations which require choosing a course of action from among several unsatisfactory alternatives, none of which is demonstrably superior to any of the others.

Chapter 2 will be devoted to several terms: *crime, criminal, delinquency,* and *delinquent.* It is nonsense to contend, "We already *know* what delinquency is, so why waste time trying to define it?" Delinquency may have various definitions, each of which would imply different research and action programs. The question posed here is what changes are most desired by our society regarding serious deviant behavior. If crime cannot be entirely eliminated, would we be most satisfied with a reduction in the overall crime rate, in the rate of serious crimes, or in the rate of crimes of violence against persons? Perhaps the public would be concerned more with criminals than with crimes and might prefer a drop in the number of first offenders or recidivists to a drop in the total number of crimes or delinquencies.

The best data available on the universe of crime and delinquency are governmental statistics regularly disseminated by the Federal Bureau of Investigation and the Federal Bureau of Prisons. These data are not without major limitations, many of which the agencies themselves clearly describe in their publications. Despite this, the data are all too often blindly used to "prove" some point or other or are dismissed as irrelevant, needlessly confirming something already known to everyone. Research constitutes the other major source of information and similarly suffers from being considered superfluous. But, as has been mentioned before, the contention that the causes of crime are already known is nonsense. Research forces us to realize how little we know. For example, many factors thought to be associated with Negro criminality are upon examination provably untrue. Thus, one recurrent theme is that Southern migrants, because of their inability to adjust to new regional ways of life, represent a disproportionate share of Negro delinquency. One study, at least, as will be seen in Chapter 3, seems to disprove this facile generalization. The belief that the percentage of non-whites in a section of a city is positively correlated with its delinquency rate is challenged by a study by Bernard Lander. Lander finds that a correlation does indeed exist but that it is curvilinear: that is, as the percentage of non-whites in a neighborhood increases, so does delinquency; but when Negroes constitute more than 50 percent of the population, delinquency drops. Areas overwhelmingly non-white are found to have very much lower delinquency rates than areas that are half white and half non-white. The true situation is still uncertain, it must be admitted, because several recent replications of Lander's work have failed to find similar curvilinear patterns. But the point is that research uncovers new facts which require the abandoning of old ideas. The dilemma of Chapter 3 has to do with the purpose of criminological inquiry, i.e., the relationship of research to policy. The immediate and necessary applicability of scientific investigations is an important issue and worthy of some debate.

Chapter 4 will examine several systematic attempts to explain delinquent behavior. Some of the theories are based on extensive already existing bodies of evidence; others have been created on a less firm empirical base and, therefore, require additional data to support or disprove them. Among the more persuasive sociological models of delinquency in current circulation are the "anomie" models by Merton, Cohen, Sykes and Matza, and Cloward and Ohlin; the "cultural transmission" theory of Shaw and McKay; and the not easily classified explanations by Kobrin and Miller. The question is which model most closely approximates reality and therefore is the most accurate explanation of delinquency. The issue of the appropriate role of criminological theory is germane here. Should it continue to aim at nothing less than a perfect model of criminal behavior, or, on a lower level, should it be immediately productive of a possibly effective action program? The latter alternative assumes that the significant variables are in fact easily manipulable; but there may be some factors, e.g, familial ordinal position, that are unmodifiable, and some other theory may contend, as the "opportunity" model perhaps does, that nothing less than a massive change in our entire way of life is needed to reduce delinquency.

The police, as the basic source of information on crime in our society, surely must be scrutinized in any meaningful discussion of criminality. Law-enforcement agencies, studied in Chapter 5, are seen to be a visible manifestation of society's efforts to protect its citizens. The police are granted a monopoly of the legitimate use of force and represent the major bulwark against the feared criminal; it is paradoxical that they are held in such low regard by a hostile public. This negative image is a reflection of a pervasive belief that the police are corrupt and inefficient (incompetent and not very intelligent, the policeman finds law enforcement the best job to which he could aspire). The extent of these sins has been greatly exaggerated. A third criticism—police brutality (excessive and illegal use of force)—has received much publicity in recent years. The opposite of this problem—the failure to invoke arrest procedure when it is legally appropriate—is much more frequently the case and is of far greater influence on criminal statistics, yet it provokes almost no commentary. It is demonstrable that when the police exceed their legal prerogatives, they perform their duties with greater efficiency, as measured by the percentage of crimes "cleared" by arrest. Should we not, therefore, legitimate their behavior and grant them this extension of power? The price, of course, is a reduction in civil rights; so the dilemma is whether an improvement in the clearance rate warrants a decrease in constitutional safeguards.

Most of what is known of the extent and differentials of crime is derived from law-enforcement agencies; but the relationship between the criminal and those who enforce the law is similar to that between the criminal and those who administer justice. Accordingly, Chapter 6 deals with the administrative procedures whereby a person suspected of having committed a crime is found guilty in a court of law and classified as a criminal The suspect, after having been arrested, interrogated, and booked by the police, is brought to a magistrate. In cases involving serious crimes the magistrate decides on the basis of evidence submitted whether to release or hold the suspect and, if the suspect is held, the amount of bail. The prosecuting attorney may then submit the case to the grand jury. If the grand jury is convinced that the state has made a prima-facie case, it will return a bill of indictment. If at the arraignment the defendant pleads not guilty to the charges in the indictment, the trial begins; the trial will finally end with a formal verdict of guilty or not guilty.

The point of contention here goes beyond the proper limits of police power; it involves an attempt to determine the best possible balance between the constitutional rights of the individual and the state's function of protecting the general population. Recent Supreme Court decisions concerning police powers, interrogations, confessions, and right to counsel have made the problem of reconciling the maintenance of the general welfare with the right of the accused to equal justice and "due process of law" one of the most difficult issues in America today.

Finally, society must react in some manner against the criminal or delinquent; this reaction will be the topic of the last chapter. Ideally, of course, serious deviant behavior might be prevented; and numerous projects to accomplish this have been instituted over the years. One of these projects, the so-called Cambridge-Somerville program, was based on the hypothesis that a "sustained friendly ego ideal" (a "big brother") might well keep a boy from becoming a delinquent. After several years in operation the experiment seems to have failed: the treated boys did no better in terminal adjustment than the nontreated controls. Nevertheless, it was in many ways a model project, characterized by the intensive detail and scrupulous honesty of its self-appraisal.

Adults who are found guilty of having engaged in crimes are most often punished by being incarcerated. Imprisonment may serve the purpose of social revenge, or it may be based on the simple (perhaps simpleminded) conviction that criminal behavior can be permanently altered by coercion and close control. It is a sad comment on modern penology that so little is known about what effect institutionalization has on the prison population. More than 95 percent of the almost quarter of a million prisoners in the United States will one day be released; it might have been expected, then, that by this time we should have formed some clear idea of the impact of prison life on the inmates. Progress is slowly being made, and in recent years several excellent studies have been made of prisons as social communities. None of these has surpassed Gresham Sykes's perceptive examination of the inmate subculture at Trenton State Prison. Sykes deals with the problems of custody, internal order, self-maintainance, punishment, and reform; the situations under which guards can be corrupted; the pains of imprisonment, including the loss of liberty, goods, heterosexual relationships, autonomy, and security; and the "argot roles" that prisoners play. The overall impression of life in prison is one of complex social relationships and involuted human interactions.

For a few criminals society selects death as an appropriate punishment. Criminals have been executed for at least 3,500 years by being stoned, decapitated, hanged, beaten, shot, electrocuted, and gassed. Death has been inflicted for such offenses as consorting with gypsies, singing scurrilous songs, and disobeying one's parents, as well as for the major felonies that have always been capital crimes. Arguments for and against capital punishment involve heredity, cost, recidivism, errors of justice, and—most important of all—deterrence.

What the primary function of punishment should be is our final dilemma. If punishment is thought to be social revenge, society's way of "getting back" at the criminal, then the efficaciousness of imprisonment would become irrelevant and the death penalty might be considered a necessity. If, on the other hand, the purpose is to keep the criminal in restraint and suspend his activity as a member of society, strict custodial control and minimal treatment would be indicated. If reformation is the goal, then the continued existence of penal servitude would be called into question and capital punishment would be considered cruel and unnecessary. It can be seen that these concepts are mutually exclusive, so that probably only one could be held as a guide to action; but none of the concepts clearly satisfies *all* the problems posed by the existence of criminals. We are faced, then, with various inadequate alternatives.

In sum, this volume is not, and was not intended to be, a survey of the field of criminology. Several areas of singular importance— for example, prediction studies and treatment-rehabilitation programs—have been deliberately omitted. These are topics of such complexity that adequate presentations would, of necessity, be too extended for a book of this scope and purpose. The purpose of this book is simply to introduce the reader to selected concepts, data, and theories; to the way the police and the administrators of justice influence criminal statistics; to societal reactions to delinquents and criminals; and to some of the important dilemmas underlying each of these areas.

2

CRIME AND DELINQUENCY

A collectivity of people known as a society typically operates within a particular ideal code of normative behavior called culture. A member of a society is invariably granted enormous latitude as to the actions in which he may permissibly engage. Beyond this range of "free" action, however, other behavior is proscribed; if this behavior is detected and brought to public attention, it might result in the imposition of social sanctions, the certainty, nature, and seriousness of which will depend upon the nature of the harm. For violations of minor social rules, moderate punishments are incurred; the violator of somewhat more important societal values or mores, perhaps because his deviant behavior might be injurious to others, is likely to be more seriously penalized. Still more serious are forms of behavior considered so reprehensible and threatening that members of the community are explicitly and formally prohibited from engaging in them. In civilized societies, such prohibitions usually take the form of criminal codes. Under these conditions, the prohibited action (the crime) is described in detail and the punishment made explicit, and various personnel become occupationally involved within an institution of law enforcement and are assigned the tasks of detecting, apprehending, convicting, and punishing the culpable offender. The blameworthy perpetrator of a crime, once his guilt has been established within the current system of criminal procedure, is defined as a criminal and made to suffer some established form of punishment.

Within each of the several legal jurisdictions in the United States, the appropriate legislative body determines what acts will be classified as crimes and what punishments they will incur. It also constructs and, on occasion, alters the procedure whereby a person suspected of committing a crime may formally be found guilty and considered a criminal.

It would be illuminating to discover why legislators in one jurisdiction prohibit as criminal some specific behavior, while another, equally august legislative body concludes that the identical act is not very reprehensible and does not define it as a crime. Admittedly there is universal agreement that murder, rape, robbery, burglary, and some other serious actions are "wrong in themselves" (*mala in se*) and are therefore crimes; but certain acts, such as fornication (voluntary sexual intercourse between two unmarried adults), are misdemeanors in some jurisdictions, while other jurisdictions—although perhaps judging them unattractive behavior—still do not legally prohibit them. Why this nonuniformity exists, and what factors (rational and irrational) operate in the legislative decision-making processes, still remains something of a mystery.

Crime

Generally, it has been held that a crime is any act or omission prohibited by law and punishable by the state in judicial proceedings.[1] More specifically, in Anglo-Saxon law, there are five *necessary* theoretical elements in a crime:

1. *The act must involve a conscious, voluntary, external harm.* Nevertheless, the omission or neglect of legal duties will still

NOTE: Footnoted references, numbered consecutively by chapter, appear at the end of the book, pp. 116–123.

meet this criterion. Additionally, simply conspiring to commit a crime and soliciting someone to engage in a crime are themselves misdemeanors under the common law.

2. *The act must have been legally prohibited at the time it was committed.* In effect this means that if some heartless legislature decided today to make kissing a misdemeanor, kisses committed before the passage of this law could not be made criminal offenses and would not be punishable under the law. The United States Constitution forbids the Federal, state, and local governments from passing any such ex post facto laws. (art. 1, sec. 9, par. 3, and sec. 10, par. 1)

3. *The perpetrator must have had criminal intent* (mens rea) *when he engaged in the crime.* If the criminal act was "willful, wanton, or done with malice," the law assumes that criminal intent was present. It must be kept in mind that if *mens rea* was lacking, the actor *cannot* be found to be a criminal; it might even be argued that in this circumstance the act itself was not a crime. The assumption of *mens rea* is sometimes difficult for someone other than a legal philosopher to comprehend. "Statutory" rape, for example, is carnal knowledge of a girl under a specific age who has given her verbal consent. Because she is under the specified age, the law says she cannot legally grant permission. The courts are not concerned with the girl's own state of mind because, in a classic legal phrase, "the law resists for her." There are cases on record in which a man, aware that rape of any type is an exceedingly serious offense, has made careful and sincere efforts to ascertain that a girl is of the age of consent, but finds later that she is really under this age. Until 1964, under these conditions a man would probably have been convicted of the crime of rape, despite his efforts to avoid committing the crime, *mens rea* being considered present because of the willful wantonness of his action.

Mens rea is also assumed in the case of "felony-murder." In most states, if *anyone* is killed during the commission or attempted commission of a felony (with the sole exception of a co-felon killed by the victim or by a third party), the felon may be found guilty not only of the particular felony he was engaged in, but probably also of first-degree murder. This is so even if he had no weapon on his person, had no plans to kill anyone, or indeed was in no position to kill anyone if he had wanted to. For instance, an unarmed felon may have been committing a burglary inside a house when a police officer attempting to arrest his partner outside the house accidentally killed another policeman or some innocent third party. Under these conditions the burglar would almost certainly be guilty of first-degree murder. The law assumes, perhaps, that the offender in such cases has engaged in actions of so dangerous a nature that he should consider that someone may well die as a consequence: he therefore is culpable (blameworthy) for any death that results.[2]

Conversely, there are several conditions under which the law assumes that criminal intent does not and cannot occur. If the actor is below the age of culpability (under the common law this was 7 years, but some statutory enactments have raised the age to 10 years or more), if he is judged to be insane, if he was coerced into committing the act, or if the act is provably accidental, *mens rea* is deemed to be lacking; the actor is not a criminal, then, and the acts themselves are probably not crimes.

4. *There must be a causal relationship between the voluntary misconduct and the legally forbidden result.* Only rarely does this requirement pose any problem. Suppose that John deliberately aims his gun and shoots Mary in the shoulder. There is certainly a direct causal relationship between John's firing his pistol and the crimes of aggravated assault, assault with a deadly weapon, assault with intent to kill, and perhaps attempted murder. But suppose that the wound, although not very serious, requires some treatment, and that Mary dies during surgery to remove the bullet. The question now arises whether John has added felonious homicide to the other crimes with which he is charged. Was there a causal relationship between his inflicting a flesh wound and the death of his victim?

5. *There must be some legally prescribed punishment for anyone convicted of the crime.* These punishments can range enormously

from suspended sentences and fines to life imprisonment and the death penalty.

The proscribed actions that are considered crimes obviously vary not only from one jurisdiction to another but also from one time period to another. In Biblical times, for example, the Mosaic code regarded the following as capital crimes: violating the Sabbath, cursing one's parents, eating leavened bread during Passover, and oppressing the widowed and fatherless. To call these acts crimes may now seem completely absurd; yet over 2,000 years later, in colonial America, a Quaker found living in the Massachussetts Bay Colony and persons caught trading with Indians in the Virginia colony were executed as capital offenders.

There are some persistently intriguing questions which may be raised regarding what might be thought of as the metaphysic of a crime. If a criminal act is committed but never comes to the attention of any public authority, has a crime been committed? If neither "victim" nor "offender" is aware of the fact that a criminal act has taken place, has a crime been committed? There are no "answers" to these problems. If one holds that by definition a crime implies an act which must come to the notice of public authorities, then a crime has not taken place unless this condition is met. Beyond this it must be asked, Do all crimes of necessity and by definition have culpable perpetrators who in time will be convicted of these acts and called criminals?

Criminal

To this last question the answer is clearly "no." Of all crimes which become known to the police, *most* do not result in any arrest; and a very small percentage of all crimes known to the police finally result in a formal conviction in a court of law. Moreover, to call someone a criminal merely because he is accused of having engaged in a crime, or because he has been arrested or held for grand jury or even placed on trial, is, in itself, to engage in criminal behavior (slander or libel) if the man so described is not convicted.

Crime is prohibited, punishable *behavior;* the criminal is the judicially proven, culpable *perpetrator* of the crime. Countries with an Anglo-Saxon legal heritage developed a rather precise set of conditions governing what evidence is admissible in determining the guilt or innocence of an accused person. By and large, the rules seem reasonable. At an earlier time in English history, very different techniques were used to prove whether the accused was a punishable offender. The so-called ordeals were, in effect, legal trials and tests of truth. The ordeals included the hot iron (carrying a red-hot bar or wearing a pair of red-hot metal gloves), boiling water (dipping one's hand into a pot of scalding water), and fire (walking on a burning pyre). If in any of these ordeals the suspect developed blisters on his hands or feet, this was tantamount to a finding of guilt and he was instantly punished. We would assume that a near-miracle would be necessary for anyone not to be found guilty. However, in the cold water ordeal (in this ordeal the accused, bound hand and foot, was lowered into a pond; if he sank to the bottom, he was considered innocent), the basic laws of nature operated in favor of the defendant.[3] Our less barbarous contemporary rules of evidence have exactly the same function as the ordeal: proving guilt or innocence. In American jurisprudence, for minor (non-indictable) offenses the determination of guilt is made by a magistrate or justice of the peace, whereas for more serious (indictable) crimes the judge or jury in a court of record makes this decision.

It has been reiterated that if a defendant is not convicted, or the conviction is not upheld by appellate courts, he is not a criminal. Are there instances when an acknowledged perpetrator of a crime is not a criminal? Certainly this might be the case under a variety of conditions. Suppose a man comes home unexpectedly and finds that he is a cuckold; in a rage at catching his indiscreet wife and her lover *flagrante delicto,* he shoots and kills the lover. At his trial he freely confesses the homicide; but the all-male jury, sympathetic to his situation and unconsciously falling back on the specious "unwritten law" allowing a wronged husband to avenge himself on the lover, acquits him. Never having been convicted, he is therefore not a criminal; but, by their verdict, did the jury not also imply that the killing itself was not a felony? Let us look at another case.

A six-year-old child, brooding over the humiliations he imagines his parents have inflicted upon him, takes revenge by killing one or both of them. He is below the age of culpability and therefore is not legally responsible for his actions. Does this mean the killing itself was not criminal? Finally, one might cite the tragic case of Howard Unrah, who, some years ago in Camden, New Jersey, shot to death no fewer than 13 neighbors and bystanders. He would seem to have engaged in multiple felonious homicide; but he was declared insane and unable to stand trial. While he was, and remains to this day, institutionalized as a man who is extraordinarily dangerous and violent, he is still technically not a criminal. What is intriguing about the above examples is not only that the actors are for one reason or another not criminals, but on some metaphysical plane it may be argued that, because they are not or could not be convicted, their actions—while examples of reprehensible and extremely dangerous deviant behavior—are not crimes.

It is disconcerting to note that often even in serious research projects, the terms *crime* and *criminal* are used with considerable lack of precision. It seems to be often assumed that anyone who is arrested is necessarily a criminal. As these are basic concepts upon which the field of criminology is based, such casual indifference is somewhat difficult to understand.

Delinquency

If *crime* and *criminal* seem tortuous concepts, they assume pristine clarity next to the extraordinarily elusive terms *delinquency* and *delinquent*. Delinquencies are all actions legally proscribed for a child above the age of culpability and below a certain maximum age (16, 17, or 18). If a child engages in the proscribed behavior, the state, acting in place of the parent (*in loco parentis*), is obliged to treat (not *punish*) the child. Thus all crimes for which adults are liable, plus many other acts which are prohibited only to juveniles until they reach adulthood, are subsumed under "delinquency." Purely juvenile delinquencies (as opposed to juvenile crime) include such offenses as truancy, incorrigibility, and running away from home, as well as some rather trivial offenses (varying from state to state) such as use of obscene language, street-corner lounging, visiting "gaming places," and smoking cigarettes. In 1963, delinquencies most likely to result in juvenile court appearances were, in order of frequency, petty larceny, burglary, runaway, automobile theft, and ungovernability.[4] Upon attaining the arbitrarily designated age of adulthood, a boy might still be viewed as ungovernable by his parents; this might result in his being sent to a psychiatrist, but no legal action could be taken on his behalf. Once he has reached this age, he is beyond the jurisdiction of the juvenile authorities. Similarly, the continued absence of a college undergraduate from his classes might result in the dean's suggesting that he search for success and happiness elsewhere, but he could not be ordered to a local reformatory for treatment. Also, an adult who has enough money to prove he is not a vagrant and who violates none of his legal familial obligations may, at his own discretion, leave his family; and while he might suffer the slings and arrows of outraged society, he has not engaged in the punishable act of "running away."

It is difficult to understand why major felonies, minor misdemeanors, and many trivial juvenile delinquencies are all to be found under the rubric of delinquency, and why boys who have engaged in petty theft, street-corner lounging, or even smoking cigarettes may all be "treated" by being institutionalized for some period of time. Perhaps these trivial juvenile delinquencies, as distinct from juvenile crimes, are not thought to be particularly threatening to society in themselves but are assumed to be clear and certain indicators of some existing maladjustment which will, perhaps must, result either in subsequent serious juvenile crime or in adult criminality. The street-corner lounger, by this reasoning, will probably become the gangster of tomorrow, and steps must be taken *now* to prevent this from occurring. Unfortunately, what evidence is currently available does not substantiate this belief; it simply cannot be said with certainty that a boy with a history of very minor juvenile delinquencies is more likely to engage in juvenile crime or adult criminality than a comparable boy with no such delinquency record. Such a belief *seems* to make sense; but the social sciences contain a large graveyard of "commonsensical" explanations of social processes which, when subjected to adequate empirical investigation, have been found to be untrue.

Delinquent

A long and unbroken series of decisions by appellate (review) courts throughout the United States has consistently held that juvenile court proceedings are not criminal trials but a judicial process to determine whether or not a child requires some form of treatment. Accordingly, the constitutional guarantees of due process of law, fundamental in criminal court proceedings, are deemed unnecessary for a juvenile when the state acts as his parent (*parens patriae*). The simple definition of a criminal as one convicted in a court of law is, obviously, inapplicable in dealing with delinquents. A child may be formally adjudicated a delinquent by a juvenile court judge on the basis of hearsay evidence (which would be inadmissible in a criminal court) or even if his delinquency has not been proved "beyond a reasonable doubt" (a crucial criterion in criminal procedure), because the rights of defendants in criminal proceedings are inapplicable here.

Even if the enormous procedural and ideological differences between juvenile and criminal proceedings are disregarded, the number of adjudicated delinquents does not represent the total of juvenile offenders in the same way that the number of convicted criminals represents the total number of adult criminals. Criminal procedure will be examined in detail later (Chapter 6), but it should be noted here that if sufficient evidence is available indicating that an adult suspect is *likely* to be a criminal (i.e., if the state has made a prima-facie case), the suspect may not legally be released without punishment except by a court finding of "not guilty." Delinquents, on the other hand, may be summarily dealt with by persons other than judges of juvenile courts, e.g., juvenile aid division officers and probation officers. In many jurisdictions, such persons are legally empowered to release a child at their own discretion before he is legally adjudicated a delinquent by the juvenile court, even if he has unquestionably been delinquent (for example, even if he has been caught in the act or has confessed or has been identified by numerous witnesses). Thus adults convicted of crimes, by and large, do represent our criminal population; but adjudicated delinquents represent only a certain percentage of youths who have provably engaged in delinquencies. Court-adjudicated delinquents represent a residual category of those juveniles who have committed delinquencies and whom the police, probation workers, and others have decided not to release.

Crime or Violation of Conduct Norms

To summarize: a *crime* is an act or omission legally prohibited by the state, which prosecutes and punishes the blameworthy offender; a *criminal* is a culpable perpetrator of a crime who is found guilty of his offense in a court of law; *delinquency* includes all acts which if committed by an adult would be crimes, plus other actions prohibited to juveniles only as long as they remain below an arbitrary statutory age; and a *delinquent* is a juvenile who has engaged in a delinquency which results in some official record and for which he has been or could have been adjudicated a delinquent in juvenile court.

These definitions are consistent with what has been termed a legalistic approach, in which the fundamental premise is that the main object of criminological concern is crime and the proven violator of the law. It must be admitted that this view is not shared by all contemporary criminologists. Prof. Thorsten Sellin of the University of Pennsylvania, in his book *Culture Conflict and Crime*,[5] suggests that the main concern of criminology is the study not of crimes but of the violation of conduct norms. He contends that every adult human being is aware of the normal (acceptable, right) manner of reacting to various situations within his society. Of course, what constitutes correct behavior differs from culture to culture; but some system of appropriate conduct norms is to be found universally, and conduct norms, unlike crimes, are not the creature of any one normative group and are not necessarily embodied in the law. In effect, it is held that violations of the criminal law are an artificial and arbitrary criterion of criminality; our interest should focus on all those antisocial actions which conflict with the "general social interest," whether or not they are technically crimes or delinquencies.

This argument was attacked by Prof. Paul Tappan,[6] a lawyer-sociologist, who asked: Precisely what are the "social interests" which when violated are worthy of study? To what extent must those interests be violated before the deviant act is an instance of "antisocial behavior" sufficiently serious to be worthy of study? If the legal approach in criminology is abandoned, are we not left without any appropriate definition of what is "injurious"? There are then no standards; and the nonlegal view, almost by definition, substitutes the value judgments of the investigator for the codified criminal law.

Additionally, when operational definitions of *delinquent* or *delinquency* are substituted for legal ones, they are frequently found upon close examination to be very fuzzy indeed. Thus, in a rather important recent study, Professors Hathaway and Monachesi of the University of Minnesota examined police and juvenile court records for information on the delinquency status of their 15,000 subjects.[7] But these legal records were *not* the basis for classifying a particular child as delinquent or nondelinquent; rather, ratings were made by field workers on a basis of "all data." Consequently, in some cases (how many is not revealed) subjects were rated delinquent without any official record of delinquency, and, conversely, some subjects were rated nondelinquent despite the existence of a court or police record. There is no description of what experiences or training enabled the field workers to make such judgments. No convincing argument is offered as to why this technique is in any way superior to the judicial definition of delinquency.

Another research project, carried out by Prof. F. Ivan Nye, examined the subtle and complex relationship between family life and delinquency.[8] Information was gathered concerning 23 different types of deviant behavior; from these, seven types, equally weighted, were used to construct a Delinquency Index. Unfortunately, the seven chosen items did not all involve violations of the law; Nye admits, for example, that neither "skipping school without a legitimate excuse" nor "defying parents to their face" (and has there been a child of this century who has not engaged in that behavior?) is a crime (or delinquency). One might even question the delinquent nature of several of the other five deviancies. Thus we are told that "purchasing or drinking beer, wine, or liquor" (including drinking at home) is a criminal offense, yet it is unclear what statute is violated when a child drinks alcoholic beverages as food or for sacramental purposes within his own home.

Dilemma

Once we have attained something approaching consensus on a basic deviant terminology and then on adequate conceptual definitions, we come face to face with a major, not easily soluble, dilemma of appropriate conventional societal goals concerning these undesired deviant actions. The dilemma has to do with what changes in crime and delinquency are most desired by the general public. This is much more difficult to determine than casual reflection would suggest, because it is certain that under no foreseeable set of circumstances will it be possible to eliminate deviant behavior completely. We are thus confronted with the necessity of choosing from among several incomplete goals. And none of these seems clearly a better goal than the others.

Deliberately avoiding at this time the central concern of criminology, the causes of crime and delinquency, the present discussion will be restricted to juvenile delinquents and delinquency and to the question, "What should we do about delinquency?" It is imperative that we determine our major *attainable* goals, for certainly different objectives require different strategies and programs.

If we are primarily concerned with the *acts* of delinquency, do we want most of all a reduction in the *total number* of delinquencies? This, of course, is the view of the mass media, which constantly inform a somewhat naïve public that delinquency rates have risen 5, 10, or 15 percent over the previous year. Most delinquencies, however, are of a trivial nature; thus fewer incorrigibilities, truancies, street-corner loungings, etc., would sharply decrease the total amount of delinquency in an area. Perhaps even more important, then, is a reduction in what we have called juvenile crimes, representing more serious acts but constituting only a minority of all recorded delinquencies. Finally, greatest concern might be for a reduction in juvenile acts of violence against the person, which, while comparatively few in number, represent the most personally threatening and fearsome of deviant acts. What, then, should our objective be: fewer total delinquencies, fewer juvenile crimes, or fewer serious, violent delinquencies?

It does not follow that the number of delinquencies equals the number of delinquents known to the authorities. A single delinquency may involve a dozen delinquents; a single delinquent might well engage in multiple offenses. A powerful case can be made for focusing our interest and limited resources not on delinquent behavior but on the delinquent himself. The problem then becomes, should present and future delinquency programs be evaluated by their ability to reduce the total number of delinquents, the number of delinquents committing juvenile crimes, or the number of delinquents who engage in violent, personal offenses?

To put the matter in its simplest terms, one must accept as given the extreme unlikelihood that delinquency can be completely eliminated and the fact that monies, facilities, and talent available to deal with delinquency are sharply limited. Rationally, then, these resources should be concentrated in the specific area of our greatest concern. Further, although there is no "right" answer to the question of where we can use our restricted resources to best advantage, some decision, some ordering of priorities, must be made. The nature of this arbitrary decision considerably affects the other dilemmas that will be dealt with subsequently in this book.

SOURCES OF INFORMATION:

statistics and research

STATISTICS

In this chapter, several of the major sources of information forming the basis of what we *know* (not intuit, speculate, guess, or contend) about criminal and delinquent behavior will be examined. Accordingly, we must be concerned with statistics, not opinions.

Governmental statistics are extraordinarily valuable in the light they shed on crime and criminals in the United States. With all their limitations (which will be discussed in detail later), these continuing, extensive bodies of data are absolutely essential in any meaningful attempt to analyze the phenomena of crime.

Uniform Crime Reports

Crimes Known to the Police   Of the myriad functions performed by the Federal Bureau of Investigation, perhaps the most important to those seriously interested in the problem of crime is its role as a central collection agency for a huge number of reports on arrests and on crimes known to the police, voluntarily submitted by many law-enforcement agencies from all parts of the country. Since 1930, the

F.B.I. has published the collated and summarized results as the *Uniform Crime Reports*. The information is disseminated, one supposes, to indicate the extent of criminality at a given point of time, to demonstrate changes in crime rates from one year to another, and to show relative differences among jurisdictions in crimes known to the police and arrest rates. For 1963, the *Uniform Crime Reports* reports a total of 2,259,081 "major" offenses (murder and nonnegligent manslaughter, forcible rape, robbery, aggravated assault, burglary, larceny of over $50, and automobile theft) in the United States, or a rate of 1,198.3 major offenses per 100,000 inhabitants. Between 1958 and 1963 the *number* of major crimes increased 40 percent, while the *crime rate* (the number of offenses per 100,000 population) increased 30 percent; the total population of the United States rose 8 percent in this 5-year period. Violent crimes (murder, rape, robbery, and aggravated assault) rose 22 percent; property crimes rose 43 percent. The perceptive reader of the *Reports* will note, however, that these are in reality only "estimated" figures, which are tabulated on the basis of data voluntarily supplied by many, but not all, law-enforcement agencies in the United States. For each state, the Federal Bureau of Investigation determines the percentage of the population for which it has received "hard" data (from local police forces), and from this it extrapolates a rate for the entire population of the state. This does not immediately recommend itself as the best possible technique for ascertaining the full extent of crimes known to the police; for, as will presently be seen, some rather peculiar results arise from this procedure. Nevertheless, this total of Crimes Known to the Police is probably, as Professor Sellin has stated, the best index of *crime* that we have. If we are interested in the *criminal,* we must use other types of data (see the subsequent discussion on *National Prisoner Statistics*).

Arrests The *Uniform Crime Reports* presents data on crimes known to the police that were "cleared" by arrest. The clearance rate, of course, varies according to the crime. Thus, in 1963, of 8,500 criminal homicides known to the police, in 91 percent of the cases someone was arrested for the offense; the clearance rate for rape was 69 percent; for robbery, 39 percent; and for burglary, 27 percent. For criminal homicides, statistics show that 12 percent were "felony-murders" (someone, usually the victim or a third person, was killed during the commission of or attempt to commit a felony); 51 percent resulted from arguments with a person not in the offender's family but usually an acquaintance; 31 percent were willful killings within a family unit (often the killing of one's spouse); the remainder were those for which the motive and offender were unknown. The victims were usually male, and almost half were between 20 and 40 years old. Those suspected of committing the offense and arrested were most often males aged 20 to 29; in over half of the cases they were Negro. Keep in mind these data relate only to persons who are suspected of having committed the crime; obviously, the number of persons actually convicted is very much smaller. For murder and nonnegligent manslaughter, the *Uniform Crime Reports* indicates that of 2,458 persons arrested, 77.2 percent were formally charged, 33.6 percent were found guilty, 16 percent were guilty of a lesser offense than the charge, 19 percent were acquitted and dismissed, and 5 percent were sent to juvenile court.

About 1,376,000 serious offenses known to the police of 1,679 cities (with a total population of slightly over 52,000,000) produced 308,474 arrests for which additional information on subsequent disposition was available. Of those arrested, 111,010 persons were found guilty in criminal court, 36,629 were dismissed or acquitted, 106,494 were referred to juvenile court, and 54,341 were apparently never brought to trial. Thus it would seem that for almost 1,400,000 crimes known to the police, less than one in ten (111,000) resulted in someone's being found guilty in a criminal court.

Criminal Careers   Perhaps because of an increasing interest in typologies—or, more fashionably, criminal behavior systems—the *Uniform Crime Reports* in 1963 introduced a new type of analysis, entitled "Careers in Crime," wherein the F.B.I. criminal identification records are utilized to present the complete criminal history of offenders reported in a given year. Of the 56,000 offenders studied, 75 percent had two or more arrests, 93 percent were males, 73 percent were white, 29 percent were under 24 years of age, and 66 percent had been arrested for the first time before age 24. The F.B.I.'s profile of the "average" sex criminal arrested in 1963 showed his age to be 35; he was 21 when first arrested for any criminal offense and 26 when first arrested for a sex crime. He had been arrested eight times during his career and had usually received some degree of "leniency" from the courts at some point in his criminal career— leniency being described as probation, suspended sentence, parole, or conditional release. The robber, burglar, automobile thief, and forger, however, were even more likely to have received lenient court treatment.

Urban-Rural and Regional Crime Differences   Because there exists a large and consistent body of evidence demonstrating the importance of urbanization as a crucial variable in criminal behavior, the *U.C.R.* presents crime and arrest rates for population centers classified as Standard Metropolitan Statistical Areas (S.M.S.A.), Other Cities, or Rural Areas. It is important to note that law-enforcement agencies which voluntarily submitted data to the Federal Bureau of Investigation represent 98 percent of all people living in S.M.S.A., 91 percent of those in Other Cities, and only 77 percent of those in Rural Areas.

The S.M.S.A. total crime rate was 1,501 per 100,000 population; for Other Cities it was 815; and for Rural Areas, 492. Rural Areas had the highest rates of murder and manslaughter, but the S.M.S.A. had the highest rates for every other offense. Further, the larger the city, the higher its overall crime rate; when cities are classified by population as "over 250,000," "100,000 to 250,000," etc., the pattern appears consistently, with the only exception being a small one due to increasing crime in the suburbs.

When regional variations are examined, it is—surprisingly—not New England but the East South Central States (Alabama, Kentucky, Mississippi, and Tennessee) that produce the lowest crime rate. The Pacific States, on the other hand, have the highest total criminality. Information presented on a state-by-state basis shows Nevada with the highest overall crime rate, and Mississippi with the lowest. Vermont has the lowest rate for murder and aggravated assault, New Hampshire the lowest rate for rape, Maine the lowest rate for robbery, and Mississippi the lowest rate for burglary, larceny, and auto theft.

Sex Examination of 4,510,835 arrests (from law-enforcement agencies representing over 125,000,000 people in 1963) reveals that 513,851 (11 percent) involved females. Of those arrested only for serious felonies, the female percentage is still only 12 percent. The percentage of women arrested for each of the following offenses is higher than their overall arrest average: for theft, women accounted for 19 percent of all arrests; for criminal homicide, 18 percent; and for aggravated assault, 14 percent. They are far less likely to be arrested for robbery (5 percent of all arrests for robbery), burglary (4 percent), auto theft (4 percent), and, of course, rape (none). For minor offenses, women account for 78 percent of all prostitution arrests, 18 percent of embezzlements and frauds, 14 percent of narcotics arrests, 13 percent of liquor arrests, 9 percent of arrests for drunkenness, 8 percent of gambling arrests, and 5 percent of all arrests for weapons offenses.

Age The statistics on age and criminality in Table 1 were taken from the *Uniform Crime Reports* for 1963.[1]
The table shows that persons under 18 were arrested for only 17 percent of all crimes reported by almost 4,000 police forces but were apprehended for over 46 percent of the seven serious offenses that preoccupy the Federal Bureau of Investigation. Persons under 25 were arrested for 37 percent of all crimes and 72 percent of the seven serious offenses. The crimes most frequently committed by persons under 25 include forcible rape (62 percent of all arrests for that offense), robbery (66 percent), burglary (78 percent), larceny (73 percent), auto theft (88 percent), stolen-property offenses (59 percent), weapons offenses (51 percent), violations of liquor laws (64 percent), and miscellaneous activities (61 percent). Conversely, the crimes for which persons over 25 are most likely to be arrested include drunkenness, drunken driving, gambling, embezzlement and

fraud, offenses against the family, vagrancy, and criminal homicide. Clearly we have here considerable support for the belief in the disproportionately high criminal behavior of youth (as measured by arrests), especially in the area of the most serious felonies.

Race   The final variable to be dealt with, race, is a major one for the purposes of this chapter. The arrest statistics by race, Table 2, supply fascinating data on this highly contentious topic.[2]

Negroes constitute about 10 percent of the population of the United States, and yet Table 2 shows that Negroes are arrested for 28 percent of all crimes and 33 percent of the seven major offenses. Negroes are arrested for murder and nonnegligent manslaughter at a rate 5.5 times their percentage of the general population. Similarly, 55 percent of all arrests for aggravated assaults, 53 percent of arrests for robbery, 47 percent of arrests for rape, and 29 percent of arrests for burglary involve Negroes. Of the remaining, less serious offenses, Negroes had a particularly high arrest rate for gambling (71 percent); they were also arrested at a disproportionately high rate for "suspicion." Examination of the *Uniform Crime Reports* reveals this last "crime" is in actuality no offense at all but rather is a vague term used to mask some clearly illegal police action. "Suspicion" is defined as "arrests for no specific offense and release without formal charges being placed."[3]

Any analysis of the criminality of Negroes must be extraordinarily complex; it would therefore be foolhardy to form, simply on the basis of these statistics, any firm conclusions on racial variations in crime rates. Some of the elements associated with Negro delinquency and crime will be dealt with in Chapter 5.

The *Uniform Crime Reports* is our major source of national statistics on crimes and arrests; but there does not exist, at the present time, a comparable compilation of data for our other object of concern: the criminal. No governmental agency is currently engaged in the collection and collation of court statistics, which, of course, are our only source of information on the universe of persons convicted in a court of law of illegal actions—i.e., criminals. We will examine governmental publications relating to prisoners; but we

Table 1   Total Arrests of Persons Under 18, Under 21, and Under 23 Years of Age, 1963
(3,985 agencies; 1963 estimated population 125,760,000)

Offense charged	Total	Number of persons arrested			Percentage		
		Under 18	Under 21	Under 25	Under 18	Under 21	Under 25
TOTAL	4,510,835	788,762	1,210,519	1,669,861	17.5	26.8	37.0
Criminal homicide:							
(a) Murder and non-negligent manslaughter	6,080	477	1,135	2,041	7.8	18.7	33.6
(b) Manslaughter by negligence	2,725	199	568	1,072	7.3	20.8	39.3
Forcible rape	9,461	1,656	3,849	5,825	17.5	40.7	61.6
Robbery	37,836	9,963	17,177	24,830	26.3	45.4	65.6
Aggravated assault	68,719	9,473	16,714	26,259	13.8	24.3	38.2
Burglary—breaking or entering	170,160	85,151	112,691	133,522	50.0	66.2	78.5
Larceny—theft	314,402	160,089	200,328	229,014	50.9	63.7	72.8
Auto theft	85,839	54,417	68,076	75,520	63.4	79.3	88.0
Subtotal for above offenses	695,222	321,425	420,538	498,083	46.2	60.5	71.6
Other assaults	184,243	22,975	41,058	67,255	12.5	22.3	36.5
Embezzlement and fraud	53,208	1,336	4,670	12,182	2.5	8.8	22.9
Stolen property; buying, receiving, etc.	15,014	4,314	6,647	8,883	28.7	44.3	59.2
Forgery and counterfeiting	30,610	2,497	6,292	11,592	8.2	20.6	37.9
Prostitution and commercialized vice	26,124	586	3,496	10,597	2.2	13.4	40.6
Other sex offenses (includes statutory rape)	59,530	12,518	18,997	27,113	21.0	31.9	45.5
Narcotic drug laws	29,604	1,880	5,697	12,589	6.4	19.2	42.5
Weapons; carrying, possessing, etc.	43,454	9,077	15,233	21,970	20.9	35.1	50.6
Offenses against family and children	58,228	921	5,330	14,511	1.6	9.2	24.9
Liquor laws	130,460	28,152	73,543	83,751	21.6	56.4	64.2
Driving while intoxicated	214,913	1,473	10,664	32,589	.7	5.0	15.2
Disorderly conduct	489,841	73,240	135,365	200,007	15.0	27.6	40.8
Drunkenness	1,510,121	18,446	69,244	171,033	1.2	4.6	11.3
Vagrancy	141,773	11,348	26,653	41,423	8.0	18.8	29.2
Gambling	102,977	1,825	5,681	15,519	1.8	5.5	15.1
All other offenses, except traffic	632,518	254,494	321,333	385,675	40.2	50.8	61.0
Suspicion	92,995	22,255	40,078	55,089	23.9	43.1	59.2

Table 2   Total Arrests by Race, 1963

(3,951 agencies; 1963 estimated population 116,952,000)

Offense charged	Total	Race					
		White	Negro	Indian	Chinese	Japanese	All others (includes race unknown)
TOTAL	4,259,463	2,943,148	1,186,870	101,253	1,817	2,640	23,735
Criminal homicide:							
(a) Murder and non-negligent man-slaughter	5,338	2,288	2,948	53	1	3	45
(b) Manslaughter by negligence	2,565	2,019	505	17	4	1	19
Forcible rape	8,457	4,402	3,935	50	2	4	64
Robbery	32,817	15,002	17,365	257	10	20	163
Aggravated assault	57,723	25,298	31,666	405	46	29	279
Burglary—breaking or entering	156,279	107,484	46,051	1,250	65	142	1,287
Larceny—theft	297,472	205,138	87,352	2,371	227	244	2,140
Auto theft	78,758	57,704	19,412	864	49	77	652
Other assaults	173,039	103,062	67,423	1,260	62	66	1,166
Embezzlement and fraud	50,680	42,904	7,333	246	12	18	167
Stolen property; buying, receiving, etc.	12,648	8,282	4,145	131	7	6	77
Forgery and counterfeiting	28,180	22,947	4,818	273	9	18	115
Prostitution and commercialized vice	22,731	11,159	11,315	120	14	20	103
Other sex offenses (includes statutory rape)	54,835	39,159	14,696	278	47	68	587
Narcotic drug laws	20,760	13,003	7,485	56	29	30	157
Weapons; carrying, possessing, etc.	40,419	19,605	20,285	205	28	17	279
Offenses against family and children	57,062	39,157	17,082	522	23	9	269
Liquor laws	124,111	91,527	29,791	2,231	21	68	473
Driving while intoxicated	207,713	172,866	31,129	2,939	60	121	598
Disorderly conduct	414,046	262,870	144,557	4,562	140	91	1,826
Drunkenness	1,501,840	1,078,427	344,585	72,720	423	505	5,180
Vagrancy	138,923	98,526	35,680	3,711	32	101	873
Gambling	75,017	18,159	53,417	31	245	482	2,683
All other offenses, except traffic	605,648	438,890	155,878	5,787	209	491	4,393
Suspicion	92,402	63,270	28,017	914	52	9	140

must be aware of the fact that prisoners represent only a portion of all convicted offenders, many of whom receive suspended sentences, fines, or probation, and are not institutionalized.

Characteristics of State Prisoners

An irregular publication of the Federal Bureau of Prisons in their National Prisoner Statistics series, *Characteristics of State Prisoners* (1960),[4] gives considerable data on prisoners received, felons first released, and the year-end prison population for 1960.

Of the 69,239 felons received by the various state institutions in 1960, 96 percent were male, 65 percent white, and 45 percent were single. The most usual offenses for which prisoners were committed were burglary (28 percent); embezzlements, fraud, and forgery (15 percent); larceny, not including auto theft (13 percent); and robbery (11 percent). Thirty-four percent received flat or definite sentences (their median sentence being 41.8 months); 62 percent received indeterminate sentences (the average *maximum* being 101.4 months).

The prison felon population in 1960 was 177,703. By and large, the basic demographic characteristics of this population closely approximate the prisoner profile given by the data for new felons. Major differences occurred, however, in median sentence lengths, which for the year-end prisoners came to 97.6 months for those having definite sentences and 148.8 months for those having indeterminate sentences. Of the year-end prisoners, 49 percent had one or more previous prison commitments; and this figure probably understates the true situation, because some states define "prior commitment" as meaning prior commitment within their own jurisdiction.

Of the 65,201 felons released in 1960, 60 percent left on parole, having served an average of 21 months; this figure was the same as those for the 1951, 1954, and 1957 populations. Persons sent to prison under definite sentences served on the average 17 months of 42-month sentences (40 percent); prisoners with indeterminate sentences served 23 months of 87-month (maximum) sentences (26 percent). Of course, all three sets of statistics demonstrated enormous regional and state variations.

It can be seen that prisoner statistics generally support arrest data on such variables as sex (females are 11 percent of those arrested and 3 to 4 percent of all prisoners), age (youth is the time of greatest criminality), and race (Negroes accounted for 28 percent of all arrests and 35 to 39 percent of the institutional population).

Limitations to Uniform Crime Reports

Most usually the *Uniform Crime Reports* is used to demonstrate variations in criminality between jurisdictions and within a jurisdiction from one time to another. The newspapers often seize on the data and "explain" all changes in offense statistics as reflections of higher (or lower) crime rates. Their rationale may be an assumption that crimes known to the police represent the total of all crimes committed. No one seriously questions the right of the press to report on crime and criminal statistics; but the manner of presentation is often oversimplified, and there is often a failure either to grasp or to communicate the cautions with which the data must be used. This has resulted in a tragically misinformed public. On reflection, however, it should be obvious that changes in crimes known to the police may arise from a variety of conditions, including changes in public opinion (e.g., the public may become less tolerant of some minor offense and, accordingly, more likely to report it to law-enforcement authorities), and alterations in certain demographic characteristics of a community (e.g., sex ratio, age composition, and degree of urbanization). Similarly, changes in the law-enforcement agencies (e.g., an increase in the number of policemen, improvement in training of the police, and variations in administrative policies and directives), may also account for fluctuations in crimes known to the police.

The *Reports,* further, must not be taken as *proving* a high rate of Negro criminality, the criminality of youth, or even regional variations in criminal behavior. The *Uniform Crime Reports* is not generally regarded as merely one more *governmental* publication; being a product of the Federal Bureau of Investigation, it has acquired some of the almost sacrosanct status of that organization.

Nevertheless, an objective evaluation reveals a number of problems relating to these crime and arrest statistics.

Problems Relating to Variations in the Criminal Law　Because there does not exist a uniform criminal code throughout the country, many actions are classified as crimes in some jurisdictions but not in others. Fornication, for example, is not a crime in 10 states; one would therefore suppose that the "Other Sex Crimes" rate would be lower in these jurisdictions than in those states where fornication is a criminal offense.

Moreover, even when there is agreement on the criminal nature of an act, very often there is no agreement on whether the crime is a felony or a misdemeanor. For example, possession of burglary tools is a felony in about half of the United States and a misdemeanor in the other half. This sort of disparity affects crime and arrest statistics; it will be shown in Chapter 5 that police reaction to a crime is to a considerable extent determined by whether the crime is arbitrarily defined as a felony or a misdemeanor. The police have a much greater power of arrest for felonies than for misdemeanors. Perhaps even more important, the "clearing" of felonies by arrest represents the basic means by which the police justify their occupational existence to a frequently hostile public. We can, therefore, properly assume that in those jurisdictions where a specific crime is a felony a larger proportion of the crimes known to the police will result in some arrest than in those areas where the same behavior is a misdemeanor.

Problems with Police (and F.B.I.) Practices　The Federal Bureau of Investigation, acting primarily as a collecting and collating agency with regard to the *Uniform Crime Reports,* is aware of the enormous variation in the accuracy and completeness of the crime and arrest figures it receives from several thousand police departments. If the records of a particular city are found to be seriously flawed, they are dropped from the *Reports* until they are demonstrably improved. Even so, there are inevitably many errors; the F.B.I. therefore specifically states that it does not vouch for the accuracy of the data submitted.

As was indicated earlier in this chapter, law-enforcement agencies voluntarily submit their statistics to the Federal Bureau of Investigation. Not all police forces respond; and rather than present limited information, the F.B.I. extrapolates these data so as to produce figures which supposedly represent *all* crimes known to the police. Thus if the F.B.I. received reports from law-enforcement agencies servicing 90 percent of the population of a state, it would increase their total statistics by 10 percent. The assumption is that the figure thus arrived at would represent the sum of all crimes known to the police in that state, as if *all* the law-enforcement agencies had submitted reports.

These projections have comparatively little effect on the overall data when 85, 90, or 95 percent of the law-enforcement agencies within a state have submitted reports. But the results obtained are questionable when a state has demonstrated extreme underreporting. It was mentioned earlier in this chapter that Mississippi is shown to have the nation's lowest rate of crimes known to the police, as well as the lowest rates of burglary, larceny, and auto theft. This may be due to a combination of undetected (and unsuspected) anticriminogenic elements existing in Mississippi, which set it apart from its more criminal neighbors. Some extensive manipulation of the statistics reveals, however, that Mississippi police reporting their data to the F.B.I. serviced only 45 percent of the state population. This was by far the lowest reporting rate for any state in the nation. Thus it is quite likely that Mississippi's low rates are directly related to this heavy underreporting. In extrapolating the data received, the totals had to be increased 130 percent; the final figures, then, are extremely doubtful and must call into question the implicit assumption that unreported segments of the population demonstrate proportionately the same crime experiences as reported areas.

Comparing crimes known to the police with arrest figures, one is struck by the relatively few crimes ending with the arrest of some suspect. In 1963, of 1,375, 969 offenses known to the police of 1,679 cities (with a population of 52,329,000), about 23 percent were cleared by arrest. The percentage producing some arrest, of course, varies by offense: 92 percent of all murders and nonnegligent man-slaughters, 72 percent of all rapes, 41 percent of all robberies, and 19 percent of all larcenies.[5] It is extremely unlikely that those arrested are in any way representative of all persons who could or should have been arrested for the non-cleared crimes.

Problems of Interpretation The *Uniform Crime Reports* explicitly warns the reader that *demographic variation* among jurisdictions is important in explaining differentials in crime rates and yet is not (and perhaps could not be) taken into account in the presentation of the data.

Another problem is that of *the relationship of crime in the universe to crimes known to the police*. Obviously, not all actions that might be crimes if they came to the attention of the proper authorities do become known to the police. "Crime in the universe" is a phrase used to denote this total of possibly criminal acts. "Crimes Known to the Police" represents an unknown (and unknowable) percentage of all possible crimes. Crimes known to the police, which result from complaints or police detection, are the best source of data we have. It is conjectured that a few crimes have very high reportability, that is, most or perhaps all of them come to the attention of the police; such offenses include assault and battery on a police officer, purse-snatching, and bank robbery. Other crimes—such as kidnapping and murder—have, perhaps, somewhat lower reportability. And it is thought that many crimes—such as fraud, blackmail, petty theft, fornication, adultery, etc.—are very infrequently brought to the attention of law-enforcement agencies. Professor Sellin has argued that a crime will have high reportability if it is of a public nature, if it induces the victim to aid the police, and if it violates a major social sentiment.[6]

Is there *any* knowable relationship between crimes in the universe (CU) and crimes known to the police (CKP)? If it could be demonstrated, first of all, that the relationship between the two is

1:1, that is, every crime committed becomes known to the police, we would be able to say that the two are identical and changes in CKP from one time period to another would exactly reflect identical changes in the number of all crimes committed. Certainly this is not the case. If, next, it could be shown that there is a fixed and known ratio between CU and CKP—so that, for example, for every five murders committed two came to the attention of the police (the ratio would then be 5:2)—any variations in CKP rate of murder would indicate exactly the changes taking place in the total number of murders. But neither is this the case. Finally, if there were a fixed but unknown relationship between CU and CKP (e.g., X:1, 5X:5), we would never know the exact relationship between the two but a change in CKP would indicate that a proportionate change was occurring in CU. Neither is this true, however. There is in fact no reason to believe that CU bears *any* constant relationship to CKP.

It must be borne in mind that Federal statistics show only total arrests and not the number of different persons arrested. How much the *multiple arrests* of a highly recidivistic individual increase the arrest figures (particularly for such crimes as drunkenness—the single largest arrest category and the single largest crime known to the police—and drunken driving) is only conjectural.

Of crucial importance is the fact that *arrest is not the equivalent of the finding of guilt.* As has been repeatedly mentioned, under our system of law one is not a criminal until he has been formally convicted in a court of law. An arrest is merely the legal apprehension of someone whom the police reasonably *suspect* is an offender, but the final decision whether he is guilty beyond a reasonable doubt is left to other authorities. In actual practice, of course, conviction rates vary considerably by region, state, and locality.

Limitations to National Prisoner Statistics

Although data on prisoners, almost by definition, have fewer limitations than the *Uniform Crime Reports,* there are still some qualifications that must be noted concerning them.

First, only comparatively few of all crimes known to the police result in the imprisonment of convicted offenders. A major study by C. C. Van Vechten in 1939 found that, on the average, of 100 major crimes known to the police fewer than six ended in conviction and fewer than four resulted in institutionalizations.[7] More recent statistics do not permit a point-by-point comparison with the findings of the Van Vechten study. Nevertheless, the *Uniform Crime Reports* for 1963 shows that of 1,375,969 offenses known to law-enforcement agencies, 23 percent were cleared by arrest and somewhat less than 9 percent resulted in convictions in criminal courts (about 8 percent were referred to juvenile courts). No information was given on the percentage resulting in imprisonment.[8]

Second, there is no fixed ratio of the number of persons institutionalized to the number of crimes committed. The ratio would vary with the number of policemen, the training of the police, the competence and training of the minor judiciary, and the decisions made by prosecuting attorneys, trial judges, juries, and other personnel in the criminal procedure.

Third, it is unlikely that the proportion of those convicted of crimes (criminals) or institutionalized (prisoners) is in any significant way representative of all those who *could* have been convicted. It has been argued that professional criminals are least likely to become prisoners because of long experience in avoiding detection and a greater likelihood of having the right political "contacts." Justice, it would seem, is not really blindfolded; and a formidable body of literature exists which proves that differential administration of justice operates at every procedural level, so that those with the least influence (Negroes, members of the lower class, etc.) are more likely to be arrested, held, tried, convicted, and imprisoned than comparable suspects with more political power.

RESEARCH

National governmental statistics on crime and delinquency produce, by necessity, a very restricted range of information. Many important —indeed crucial—aspects of criminal behavior are not, and simply could not be, dealt with at all. These statistics are of very limited use in evaluating the impact of action-treatment-punishment programs; moreover, they relate only vaguely to one of the central concerns of criminology: the etiology of criminal and delinquent behavior. By and large, what little we know about the causes of crime has been the result of a considerable number of studies which have utilized a wide range of research designs, methods of analysis, etc. It is impossible to summarize here even the most important findings in the field, but two pieces of research will be presented in some detail. Utilizing different approaches, techniques of analysis, and theoretical models of explanation, they are similar only in so far as they are attempts to find some sociological variables associated with delinquency. These two studies are Bernard Lander's investigation of delinquency in Baltimore, and a piece of research by the author on migration and delinquency. Lander's work was selected because it has produced the greatest number of replications of any recent criminological work. The migration study carried out by the author was chosen because it would permit description not only of the subject population, methodology, and results, but also of the crucial and somewhat arbitrary decisions encountered at every juncture of this research project, which are a fundamental aspect of almost any scientific investigation. The decisions and the rationales underlying them will provide, it is hoped, some insight into the nature and process of criminological inquiry.

Toward an Understanding of Juvenile Delinquency[9]

Probably the most provocative piece of criminological research of the last 20 years is Bernard Lander's study of 7,193 juveniles who were delinquent in Baltimore, Maryland, between 1939 and 1942. The rate of delinquency for white males aged 6 to 17 was 13 per 1,000, and the rate for white females was 1.9; the rate for Negro males was 44, and the rate for Negro females was 12. No statistically significant correlation was found between juvenile delinquency and population change, median education, or rental value in census tracts. Negroes, making up 20 percent of the juvenile population in Baltimore, constituted 49 percent of the delinquents. Whereas the *total* juvenile delinquency rate correlated very highly (+ .70) with the percentage of Negroes in a census tract, the correlation between

Negro juvenile delinquency and the percentage of Negroes in a tract correlated at only + .19. Upon examination it was found that the percentage of Negroes in a neighborhood and Negro delinquency rates were positively associated as the percentage of Negroes in the area increased from 0 to 50 percent; but in areas characterized by populations more than 50 percent Negro the relationship was far less strong. Thus in sections which were less than 10 percent Negro, the Negro delinquency rate was 8.1 per 1,000 Negroes; in areas 10 to 29 percent Negro the rate was 13.4; in areas 30 to 49 percent Negro it was 13.7. But in areas 50 to 69 percent Negro, the rate fell to 10.4; in areas 70 to 89 percent Negro it was 12.3; and the lowest Negro rate of delinquency—7.1—occurred in areas that were over 90 percent Negro.

By use of a statistical technique known as factor analysis, Lander demonstrated that two factors associated with juvenile delinquency were the percentage of non-whites in an area and the percentage of homeowners in an area. As has been indicated before, the correlation between Negro population and delinquency was significant but highly curvilinear, with delinquency dropping when Negroes accounted for over 50 percent of the population in an area and the greatest stabilization (nondelinquency) taking place in neighborhoods which were overwhelmingly Negro. A rather consistantly negative correlation was found between delinquency and home-ownership. Lander contended that the major factor in delinquency was anomie, and areas with the greatest social instability and normlessness (as measured by low percentage of homeowners and by greatest racial mixture) were most anomic.

Lander's study caused such a stir in criminological circles that it was followed by more replications than probably any other recent piece of criminological research.

In 1959 Bates[10] replicated Lander's work, using data from St. Louis for 1957, and found a much lower correlation between non-whites and delinquency. Apparently unable to utilize the same statistical techniques as Lander's, he used a different mode of analysis and found that in St. Louis tracts that were over two-thirds Negro had the highest delinquency rates, though these rates were not much different from those of census tracts that were 34 to 66 percent Negro. Some manipulation of his data does support the importance of lack of homeownership as a factor in delinquency.

In a later study, Bates and McJunkins studied St. Louis for the years 1958–1959 and San Diego for 1960–1961 and found that there was a positive linear (not curvilinear) correlation between delinquency and the percentage of non-whites in an area (and this relationship did not change even in areas over 50 percent Negro).[11]

David Bordua, believing that the "same census data indicators of 'anomie' and social instability may not be characteristic of other cities," examined delinquency in Detroit for 1948 to 1952 and did not find Lander's curvilinear correlation between the percentage of non-whites and juvenile delinquency.[12] No matter how he manipulated the data, his findings never displayed the "inverted U-shape" that Lander had found for Baltimore.

Kenneth Polk used data for 1950 from 84 census tracts in San Diego, California. After much analysis of the factors correlated with delinquency, he was unable to reject the hypothesis that areas with high percentages of "ethnic" populations have disproportionately high rates of delinquency; and his research did not show the relationship to be curvilinear.[13]

Conlin's doctoral thesis examined Baltimore Juvenile Court data for 1958. Whereas Lander had found a correlation of + .70 between the percentage of non-whites and the delinquency rate in census tracts, Conlin's correlation between these variables was only + .13, with delinquency being slightly higher in neighborhoods with the highest percentage of non-whites.[14]

Chilton, in his doctoral dissertation, made the most recent and careful replication. He attempted to reconcile some of the contradictory findings of Lander and Bordua concerning delinquency and anomie.[15] Accordingly, he not only reexamined Lander's findings for Baltimore and Bordua's for Detroit but he added new data for Indianapolis. His findings for all three cities did not strongly support the idea that delinquency is more closely associated with anomic factors (high percentage of non-whites and low percentage of homeowners) than with economic characteristics. Delinquency

rates within census tracts were closely related to the rate of tran-
siency, poor housing, etc. in those tracts. The percentage of owner-
occupied dwellings was significantly and negatively correlated with
delinquency in all three studies; overcrowding was important in
the Indianapolis and Detroit data but not the Baltimore data; the
percentage of foreign-born persons was crucial only in the Bordua
study, and the percentage of non-whites was important only when
Lander corrected for its curvilinear relationship with delinquency.
When Chilton remanipulated Lander's own data, the results were
somewhat different from Lander's original presentation. Chilton concluded that, when the Detroit and Indianapolis data were factor-
analysed and subjected to regression analysis, delinquency was importantly related to overcrowded housing, low income, unrelated
individuals in the household and poor education. His findings did
not support Lander's conclusion that delinquency is more closely
associated with anomic characteristics of census tracts than with
their economic characteristics.

If we accept Lander's contention that the anomic features of
neighborhoods are best measured by both the percentage non-whites
and the percentage of homeowners, none of the replications produces
findings similar to his own. It is impossible to guess at this time
what directions this mode of research will take. Certainly, it is not
too much to expect that the inevitable use of variables and techniques of analysis other than those that are census-derived may, in
time, produce results that will substantiate or refute the anomic
model of delinquency.

Delinquency and Migration[16]

Migration has always offered itself as a ready explanation for much
delinquency. Yet when the existing research is examined in detail,
the very limited nature of most of the studies makes it clear that
the matter is not settled. Additionally, a small but interesting body
of literature exists which shows a slightly negative correlation of
migration with delinquency. It seemed, therefore, that a careful
study in this area might prove profitable. After all relevant material

had been closely examined so that the more egregious errors, at least, could be avoided, several problems had to be dealt with. Juvenile court records were the best source of information on delinquency; if they were not available, the study could not be undertaken. Fortunately, after only minor difficulties, the President Judge of the Municipal Court of Philadelphia granted the author permission to examine the Philadelphia Juvenile Court files. Next, a sample of the total juvenile population had to be secured which would contain both delinquents and nondelinquents as well as adequate numbers of migrants and native-born persons. Ideally, everyone aged 7 to 18 in Philadelphia should have been sampled, but this was obviously impossible because of time and financial limitations. It was not possible to sample all school children in Philadelphia because the parochial and private-school populations were unavailable for study; and to have undertaken a cross section of even the entire public school population would have meant sampling over 200 separate schools. Before any sampling could take place, it was first necessary to have access to some extensive system of records. Some members of the Philadelphia Board of Education feared that the study might produce "anti-Negro" findings; but the local branch of the Urban League, having evinced some interest in the project, intervened with the Board, and this allowed splendid cooperation with the School Board thereafter.

To maximize the utility of the sample, the subject population were all (1) male, (2) born between 1939 and 1945, (3) attending the Philadelphia public school system in 1957, and (4) residing within a 40-block area in North Philadelphia in 1957. These criteria were established for the following reasons: (1) The male delinquency rate was at least five times the female rate. (2) By 1958, when the data were collected, the youngest of the subjects would be 13 (the beginning of the ages of high delinquency rates) and the oldest would be over 18 (and would thus have passed the age defined for delinquency). (3) The only records open for inspection were those of the public school system; the subjects therefore had to be drawn from within this system. (4) The geographical area selected had the highest delinquency rate of any area in the city; it contained a very high percentage of migrants; and it was serviced by fewer schools than any other comparable high-delinquency area.

All schools servicing the selected area were examined, and 1,062 boys were found to meet the four requirements. It must be admitted that if a boy's record showed the wrong date of birth or the wrong home address for 1957, or if he attended a school not in the normal servicing area, he would have been inadvertently omitted. A considerable amount of information for each boy, particularly regarding his full name (and variations in his surname), age, and residence, was secured from the school files. Each name and its variants was checked against several Juvenile Court record files to find which boys were delinquent.

The original temptation was to use a legal definition of delinquency and classify as delinquent only boys who were formally adjudicated delinquent juvenile court proceedings. However, a close examination of juvenile court records revealed, as has been mentioned before (Chapter 2), that many who were certainly guilty of having committed a juvenile offense (they were caught in the act or had confessed) were released, by persons legally empowered to do so, before any court action could be taken. Perhaps the most sociologically valid definition would consider a boy as delinquent if he had any juvenile court record, regardless of whether or not there had been any formal adjudication of delinquency. In Philadelphia, if the Juvenile Aid Division officer decides to "arrest" the juvenile, the boy then acquires a permanent juvenile court record, regardless of the subsequent outcome of the case. It might be argued that a boy with a juvenile court record could not easily differentiate between action taken by a probation worker and that taken by a judge (who might, after all, discharge him or place him on probation). The most important aspects of the procedure to the juvenile would be that he had been in custody, that he knew he was guilty, that "they" knew he was guilty, and that he had been warned not to commit any more delinquencies. His self-image would be one of a delinquent, and his family and peer group would similarly classify him as a delinquent. The existence or nonexistence of a court record, then, became the operational definition of delinquency used in the study.

A migrant was defined as anyone born outside the limits of the city of Philadelphia who arrived at Philadelphia at any age after birth. Obviously the best measure of migration would relate not to place of birth but to where early formative years of life had been spent. Unfortunately, this information was not available from school records, which revealed only where the pupil was born and when he entered the Philadelphia school system. Of course if a boy entered the school system after the first grade, it was then possible to determine rather precisely when he had come to Philadelphia. Most children not born in Philadelphia, however, began in the first grade in Philadelphia schools; in such cases, a migrant child could have arrived in Philadelphia a few days after birth, a few days before entering the first grade, or at any age in between, and nothing in the file would give information on this.

Analysis in depth was made only of the Negro subject population, since the white migrants in the population were very few in number (and these were usually immigrants, who presented a set of problems of adjustment quite different from those of internal migrants) and the sample produced only two Philadelphia-born Puerto Ricans.

Forty-two percent of the 890 Negroes in the population were migrant, and 34 percent (300) had juvenile court records. Of the 517 Philadelphia-born (PB), 40 percent were delinquent; whereas only 27 percent of the 373 migrants had delinquency records. This, of course, is just what one should expect. Many migrants came to Philadelphia after the age of seven and therefore were less exposed to the risk of becoming delinquent in Philadelphia (although they may have acquired delinquency records in cities they migrated from). If a boy came to Philadelphia at age 17, there would be only ones year (age 17 to 18) in which he could become a delinquent in Philadelphia; on the other hand, a boy born and raised in Philadelphia could acquire a delinquency record in any one of 11 years (ages 7 to 18). These differences could be dealt with by comparing the migrants and natives for "lengths of delinquency exposure":

from the total number of years the entire Philadelphia-born and migrant groups had resided in Philadelphia between the ages of 7 and 18, the average number of years of exposure per delinquent and per delinquency could be determined for each population. Thus, among 517 natives exposed to the risk of delinquency in Philadelphia for a total of 4,265 years, there were 200 delinquents who engaged in 537 delinquencies. This gives an average of one delinquent per 21.3 years of exposure, and one delinquency per 7.9 years of exposure. For migrants the averages were one delinquent per 26.9 years of exposure and one delinquency per 12.4 years. Migrants, it would seem, were less likely to become delinquent and committed fewer delinquencies. These findings probably tended to *understate* the negative relationship between migration and delinquency. The data were not standardized for age, and none of the 890 subjects became delinquent before the age of nine; all 517 natives, therefore, had two full years of delinquency exposure void of any delinquency (a total of 1,034 delinquency-free years); but only 61 percent of the migrants—i.e., those who came to Philadelphia by age 7—were in a similarly favorable position.

Next, there was an examination of migrants and natives equally exposed to the risk of delinquency in Philadelphia: all 517 natives were compared with the 227 migrants who arrived in Philadelphia by age 7 (and therefore could not have been delinquent elsewhere), with year of birth held constant. Table 3 shows that for those born in 1944 and 1945 there were no appreciable differences between migrants and natives. For every other age group the rate of delinquency for the native-born was considerably higher than the rate for comparable migrants. The boys in the oldest group, born in 1939 or 1940, became 18 in 1957 or 1958. This group comprises all the boys who had been fully exposed to the risk of delinquency in Philadelphia. Fully 63 percent of the Philadelphia-born boys (almost two out of three) were delinquent, as were 50 percent of the migrants. Fifty-nine percent of *all* members of the oldest group were delinquent. These figures, it is submitted, are probably the best and most accurate measure of the real delinquency potential of an area—not published court statistics showing that 5 to 10 percent of the children in a section of the city have become delinquent in a given year, nor an overall percentage of boys living in a neighborhood who have ever had a delinquency record (in this case, about 35 percent of the subject population). Certainly the most mean-

TABLE 3. Delinquency Rates of Negro Natives and Negro Migrants Residing in Philadelphia by Age 7 by Year of Birth

Year of Birth	Natives	Migrants
1945		
Number in group	103	34
Number of delinquents	19	6
% delinquent	(18.5)	(17.6)
1944		
Number in group	101	35
Number of delinquents	27	10
% delinquent	(26.7)	(28.6)
1943		
Number in group	88	39
Number of delinquents	30	7
% delinquent	(34.1)	(17.9)
1942		
Number in group	87	45
Number of delinquents	40	14
% delinquent	(46.0)	(31.1)
1941		
Number in group	65	40
Number of delinquents	38	17
% delinquent	(58.5)	(42.5)
1939–40		
Number in group	73	34
Number delinquents	46	17
% delinquents	(63.0)	(50.0)
TOTAL		
Number in group	517	227
Number of delinquents	200	71
% delinquent	(38.7)	(31.3)

ingful index is the probability of a child's ultimately becoming a delinquent when he has been fully exposed to the risk of delinquency in a neighborhood.

Regardless of the measure used (gross delinquency rates or lengths of delinquency exposure and comparison of natives with migrants coming to Philadelphia before age 7), the results produced are remarkably uniform and consistent. What is important is not the size of the differences, which are seldom statistically significant, but their regularity and consistency. How can the slightly negative relationship of migration and delinquency be explained? We might hypothesize that migrants, by greater cunning or deviousness, manage to avoid detection better than natives. Or perhaps there operates some differential administration of justice, with native-born boys being discriminated against by juvenile authorities. Neither theory is supported by any evidence. Perhaps there are relatively fewer migrant delinquents because the isolation of Negro migrants within the northern Negro ghettos provides protection from the larger Negro society. Once more, there is little supportive data for this. (Table 3 shows the differential between migrants and natives decreasing from the group born in 1943 through the group born in 1939–1940; on the other hand, the same table shows that the rates are most similar for the two youngest age categories.) The most likely explanation is that northward migration of Negroes may be a selective process, with the most disorganized families—with the most delinquency-prone children—tending to remain in the South, while the more ambitious, socially mobile, and conventional families are more likely to migrate northward.

Dilemma

"Toward an Understanding of Juvenile Delinquency" and "Delinquency and Migration" were not presented as perfect examples of criminological inquiry nor because they constitute the most important recent research. Yet Lander's study has become almost a landmark in criminology. The response to the work was almost without precedent; extensive discussions and debates and a remarkable number of replications soon followed. Beyond the relatively minor issue of whether or not its findings were "true," it has focused the attention and the creative energy of a number of criminologists on the possibility of associating delinquency with several census-derived demographic variables. In time, Lander's study may even prove instrumental in stimulating that rarest of sociological phenomenon, a series of research projects with roughly the same experimental design, producing a *consistent* body of data on the interrelationship of the same set of sociological factors. The two studies represent different kinds of research, utilizing very different methods of analysis. They reach several interesting conclusions about how certain factors are or are not related to delinquency; Lander's in fact offers a theoretical model of explanation—the "anomie" theory —for the phenomenon of delinquency. The two studies were chosen primarily to illustrate the difficulty in ascertaining on an empirical basis, the positive relationship of sociological variables and delinquency. Thus, it has been seen that the "obvious," automatically assumed criminogenic effects of migration are simply not supported by the study presented.

The dilemma here transcends the individual merit of these pieces of research; it involves the larger question of the purpose of research in criminology and, by inference, in the social sciences. The criminologist, of course, would state that the function of research is to develop systematic bodies of data from which valid generalizations can be derived either to support or disprove existing criminological theories or to aid in the creation of some new explanation. On a less ambitious level, it might be held that research often aims at uncovering groups of variables *correlated* with a particular phenomenon such as delinquency. (The problem of causal relationship will be discussed in Chapter 4.)

The general public and a considerable number of its elected representatives, however, believe that the social sciences are not really sciences at all. This generally low regard in which the social sciences are held perhaps results from a feeling that somehow certain areas are intrinsically scientific and others are not, and that when workers in the latter areas contend that their fields are sciences and that they themselves are engaged in scientific pursuits they are at once pretentious and absurd. Sociology and criminology are held to fall into this "unscientific" category. There seem to be two notions behind this belief: that sociology and criminology deal only with matters of common sense, and that human beings—their subject matter—are not susceptible of scientific study. It has been shown that criminology, so far from dealing with only common-sense matters, proves many common-sense ideas to be untrue. But can it deal scientifically with its subject matter? This seems to involve a question of ethics.

Let us examine a parallel case. Medical research is certainly considered by the public to be a true science. Accordingly, it is accepted that medical experiments necessarily involve the use of treatment and control groups. Thus, for example, when the value of a new, unproven drug is tested, children randomly placed in a control group are not given the new medication. Some of them will perhaps contract the disease the drug is supposed to prevent or cure. The results may be fatal or injurious, and possibly they might have been prevented by the drug being tested. This is, quite simply, an inevitable, if tragic, concomitant of medical research. It is a necessary, painful cost that must be paid for the advancement of science.

Consider now the case of criminology. In point of fact, we can presently do relatively little to prevent delinquency, eliminate recidivism, rehabilitate or reform. Could not the public be persuaded, in its own best interests, to regard delinquency as amenable to scientific analysis? Then we might put available energies, resources, and talents into a considerably expanded series of research projects. And we might carefully evaluate a few selected action programs by comparing samples of treated potential delinquents (or recidivists) with others forming nontreated control groups. It is true that a few members of the control groups might become official delinquents and that this might have been prevented by treatment. But control groups must be considered the necessary price required for the development and testing of the best means of protecting society and treating the child. If we are willing to accept the fact that children in medical control groups may become ill, we should accept the fact that children in sociological control groups may become delinquent. Is this a greater cost than we are able to bear? It may be that we must bear it if we are to advance at all in our ability to deal with crime.

Even if it is granted that criminology is a science of sorts—though primitive and crude—and may therefore engage in scientific pursuits, the question then arises whether there is any *need* for further criminological research. Doesn't everybody already *know* the causes of delinquency? Poverty, disorganization, discrimination and segregation, broken homes, illegitimacy, school drop-outs—even migration and racial heterogeneity—are listed as causes as if there were no possible doubt about them. The problem is that while it is clear to the professional that pitifully little is known about factors correlated with delinquency or crime—let alone causative factors—it is widely felt that to continue research is to waste precious, insufficient funds. It is felt by many that what funds we have would be better spent on something—anything—that may reduce "crime in the streets" *now*. But without research our store of information will not significantly increase, and the programs of prevention-treatment-reformation undertaken will endlessly manipulate the same sterile techniques.

It is not a particularly attractive prospect that in much research some of the subjects used as controls may become delinquent. But without research we can make no progress, for our programs could be based on incomplete or mistaken beliefs and could not possibly be successful in the long run.

SOCIOLOGICAL THEORIES
OF DELINQUENCY

There have been a number of attempts to explain the causes of crime "scientifically." It should be noted that the concept of science, until relatively recently, has been rather nebulous. Among the earliest attempts were those emphasizing physiological, biological, and genetic factors. In the sixteenth century physiognomic theories of crime were enumerated, finding, for example, that the thief was characterized by small ears, bushy eyebrows, a small nose, and mobile eyes. Three centuries later, Franz Joseph Gall and his dedicated disciples developed the science of phrenology, which was based on the belief that the contours of one's skull exactly measured the several localized functions of the brain and were directly related to his behavior. Less than 100 years ago more sophisticated, if still quite crude, methodologies were first used to "prove" the biological basis of crime. There were numerous investigations of "family trees,"[1] anthropometric measurements of prisoners and nonprisoners,[2] correlations of criminality in fathers and sons,[3] and comparisons of the criminality of monozygotic and dizygotic twins,[4] but the best current judgment is that they have all failed to establish heredity as an important factor in criminal behavior.

Psychology has had an enormous impact on the scientific world in this century; it is therefore not surprising to find that psychology has been the basis of numerous explanations of criminality. Such explanations have generally been founded on the belief that some mental disturbance is significantly more prevalent among criminals than noncriminals. It is surprising, however, that relatively few systematic models, beyond the psychoanalytic Freudian, neo-Freudian and post-Freudian speculations, have been offered.

The personality of the criminal has been variously described as typically feebleminded (subnormal in intelligence, he is unable to appreciate the meaning and purpose of the law), psychotic (he is incapable of rationally operating within his society), or psychopathic (he is unalterably engaged in repeated antisocial actions). "Emotional disturbance," an omnibus condition involving sibling rivalry, feelings of insecurity, conflict, and rejection, has often been proposed as the major cause of delinquency.[5]

Some evidence has been produced both supporting and contradicting these theories. Professors Schuessler and Cressey closely examined 113 different studies, which used 30 different personality instruments. They compared the test scores of criminals and delinquents with those of noncriminals and found that 66 (58 percent) of the studies could not differentiate between criminals and noncriminals, that several tests presumably measuring the same personality dimensions did not give similar results, and that the same test produced inconsistent findings.[6] Even more recently, there was a very careful and intensive investigation of the accuracy with which the Minnesota Multiphasic Personality Inventory, probably the best-regarded psychometric test, could successfully predict potential delinquency. The subjects were some 15,000 ninth-grade pupils in Minnesota. The M.M.P.I. did rather well, predicting delinquency correctly for 37 percent of the male and 26 percent of the female subjects. But a group of schoolteachers, asked to guess which pupils were "likely to get into trouble with the law," did even better; the schoolteachers were accurate for 45 percent of the boys and 35 percent of the girls in their sample.[7]

Almost by default, it would seem, sociological theories, emphasizing certain aspects of our social structure and organization, have become without question the most persuasive and influential models of delinquent behavior in current circulation. Attention will be paid to what have come to be called the "Anomie" theories, from Merton to Cloward and Ohlin, and to theories of "Cultural transmission." Two models, Kobrin's and Miller's, do not clearly fall into either category, and they therefore have been assigned somewhat arbitrarily to one school or the other.

Anomie

Robert K. Merton[8] In 1938, Robert K. Merton, probably the best-regarded sociologist in America today, first formulated his ideas on the social sources of deviant behavior. These ideas were to be expanded in several subsequent revisions of the classic article in which they originally appeared. There are certain aspects to American social structure, according to Merton's theory, which exert pressure upon individuals, causing some of them, under certain conditions, to engage in delinquency. This pressure is caused by the "imperfect integration" of culturally defined *goals* and acceptable, institutionalized *means* for obtaining these goals. Means and goals are often independent of one another, so that in our society most individuals internalize the great emphasis placed upon goals— upon the actual attainment of success (status aspiration) or its more concrete form, money—without equally assimilating the appropriate social norms (conventional means) for securing these goals. In effect we emphasize success and pay comparatively little attention to how it is to be secured. Antisocial behavior is often evoked by this non-integration of means and ends; for some groups, attempting to compete within the conventional rules of the game, almost by definition cannot succeed. People are asked to aspire to wealth and then are denied effective opportunities to do so legitimately. Al Capone, for example, represented the "triumph of amoral intelligence over morally prescribed failure when channels of vertical mobility are closed or narrowed in a society which places a high premium on economic affluence and social ascent for all its members."

Within such a social structure, anomie or normlessness, develops in the form of "loss of orientation" for an appreciable segment of the population, particularly those in the lower social classes. These members of the lower class cannot compete realistically in terms of established middle-class standards of worth; and values or goals are developed and retained only as long as there remains some possibility of their attainment. Members of the lower classes, therefore, frequently become anomic. In time they come to reject the old values and engage strenuously in activities aimed at eliminating their overwhelming feelings of helplessness and social isolation. In one type of reaction, called "innovation," the conventional middle-class material goals of success are maintained but the morally appropriate means of attaining these goals are rejected; the individuals create and accept a different set of values (usually illegitimate) which permit them to pass from intolerable anomic isolation to reintegration within new groups holding these new values. Obviously these new noninstitutional norms, relating to means of securing material goals, are judged by the larger society to be negative and deleterious; but they remain advantageous for those who adopt them in so far as they tend to eliminate basic feelings of insecurity.

Solomon Kobrin[9] In a very provocative article published in 1951, Kobrin states that a superficial examination of the delinquency rates of even what are thought to be the worst sections of a city seems to indicate that most boys do not become delinquent. By manipulating available data, however, he concludes that most boys in these neighborhoods *do* acquire records of juvenile delinquency before reaching adulthood.[10] He goes on to state that in high-delinquency areas delinquency is a widely diffused phenomenon, representing a type of *normative* behavior with its own system of values and institutional forms. These areas are characterized by a duality of conduct norms: the conventional society values embraced by nondelinquents, and the deviant value system of delinquent boys. These high-delinquency neighborhoods contain a mixture of boys who have been officially classified as juvenile delinquents and who will later become adult criminals, boys who engage in undetected delinquent behavior, boys with delinquency records who will not become adult offenders, and boys without police records who will subsequently become adult offenders. Why does the "reversal of career lives" take place? Perhaps it is because children in these areas frequently participate simultaneously in both the criminal and the conventional social systems, for without question there is considerable interaction among the occasional delinquents, the active and persistent delinquents, and the nondelinquents. Some children may play different and conflicting roles under different conditions—persistent delinquent, occasional delinquent, and nondelinquent—and in so doing they fully experience the alternative value systems. Over time, however, even these persons come to occupy more consistently either a conventional or a delinquent role by interacting more and more with persons who have adopted the same role traits. There occurs, in effect, progressive alienation of the two systems from each other.

Different areas demonstrate different degrees of interaction between the conventional and criminal "worlds"; in some neighborhoods there is considerable integration, whereas in others there is very little. The closest interaction occurs where adult criminality is both systematic and organized and the leaders of the criminal organizations retain, to some extent, membership within some conventional institutions. Delinquent boys are objectively appraised as to their likelihood of becoming successful offenders on the basis of their juvenile behavior. Thus delinquency is contained within this form of local structure. On the other hand, there is minimal interaction between the two systems in areas where adult crime is sporadic and unorganized. Here delinquency is unrestricted by any element of the adult social structure, and delinquents, independent of any adult control, engage in acts which are violent, wild, and seemingly irrational.

Albert K. Cohen[11] In 1955, one of the most important recent theoretical models of delinquent behavior was enunciated by Albert K. Cohen in his highly regarded book *Delinquent Boys*. The theory stems largely from Merton's theory of anomie. Cohen contends that the working-class boy faces special problems of personal adjustment, particularly in the area of status-frustration, because his lower-class socialization has trained him inadequately for achieving success (as it is measured by the dominant middle class) and has irreparably handicapped him in competition for higher status in a conventional society. In order to secure highly prized and desired rewards, the boy must compete with middle-class boys who have been more effectively socialized in the appropriate legitimate means of securing those rewards. He is involved in an economic system characterized by heavy competition for scarce rewards; and these rewards are distributed for achievements judged not by his own but by other standards of behavior and performance. These middle-class values, which are somewhat foreign to him, include favorable attitudes toward ambition, individual responsibility, skill, ability to postpone immediate gratification, ability to "get along," control of aggression, respect for property, and distrust of "change." After competing and failing, he reacts to his inevitable failure by rejecting conventional values. Gang activity within his delinquent subculture represents a solution to his psychological problems. In embracing his gang and the new values it offers him, he not only breaks with the dominant middle-class morality but is offered a means of eliminating his guilt feelings. He can eliminate guilt feelings because the mechanism of reaction-formation operates: the gang legitimizes (accepts) hostility and aggression simply because these modes of behavior are diametrically opposed to the despised (and unachievable) middle-class values. His acts and those of his gang are described as malicious, negativistic, and nonutilitarian. This behavior is particularly frightening to the larger society, which fails to comprehend what purpose it might serve. Theft, burglary, and even robbery are at least understandable because they aim at securing wealth, even though the means are illicit; vandalism, malicious mischief, and random "bopping," on the other hand, are incomprehensible.

Gresham A. Sykes and David Matza[12]   Some modification of Cohen's thesis took place as a result of Sykes and Matza's article of 1957, in which they attacked the idea that the delinquent comes to conceive of his delinquency as being "right" and that, accordingly, he suffers no guilt or shame because of his antisocial behavior. It is their belief that many delinquents do experience feelings of guilt; they cite the fact that many delinquents confess to such feelings and, beyond this, to respecting and admiring many conventional, middle-class persons. Additionally, it is suggested that delinquents categorize others as those who can be victimized (fair game) and those who should not be. If it is the case that delinquent behavior can be directed only against some disvalued social groups or persons, does this not suggest that the delinquent may believe in the "wrongfulness" of delinquency? It is doubtful that delinquents are completely unresponsive to the continual demands for conformity to conventional society. The delinquent, of necessity, attempts to justify (rationalize) his deviant behavior, and this rationalization is a *sine qua non* for the occurrence of deviant behavior. Techniques of "neutralizing" guilt may take various forms such as: (1) denial of responsibility (the delinquency is said to be an accident or due to forces beyond the control of the delinquent); (2) denial of injury (it may be said that the act is not really a delinquency, as no one was physically injured by it); (3) denial of victim (the delinquency is said to be not an indiscriminate attack or injury upon some person randomly selected, but rather an act of rightful retaliation, e.g., an attack on "degenerates"); (4) condemnation (the delinquent contends that those condemning his actions, such as policemen who often treat suspects with needless brutality, are themselves often hypocrites or deviants in disguise); (5) appeal to higher loyalties (the delinquent suggests that he is caught between the dictates of conventional society and the conflicting demands of his peer group, and it is not so much that conventional norms are rejected as that the gang norms involve a higher level of loyalty).

Albert K. Cohen and James F. Short Jr.[13] Responding to some of Sykes and Matza's elaboration of the model of delinquent subculture offered in Cohen's *Delinquent Boys,* Cohen and James Short maintain that reaction-formation certainly represents "one of the most elementary forms of neutralization." More importantly, they hold that there are a number of different delinquent subcultures (in some ways their analysis is similar to Kobrin's): (1) Parent-Male subculture (similar to the working-class delinquency pattern discussed in *Delinquent Boys*); (2) Conflict-Oriented subculture (characterized by large organized gangs engaged in considerable violence), (3) Drug Addict subculture (which eschews more violent forms of delinquency); (4) Semi-Professional Theft subculture; (5) Middle Class Delinquency subculture (with different origins and bases from those of the working-class delinquent subculture).

Richard A. Cloward and Lloyd E. Ohlin[14]   This very fashionable statement of "opportunity" theory was published in 1961. Unlike most of the other models discussed, it has become the theoretical basis for an extensive action program—Mobilization for Youth—aimed at reducing or eliminating delinquency in selected areas of New York City's lower East Side. Cloward and Ohlin hold that American culture makes the seeking of success morally mandatory but differentially distributes the legitimate (*and even illegitimate*) opportunities for achieving success. The lower-class boy strives to reach the common goals by conventional means; because he is doomed to fail, he is attracted to the delinquent subculture, which legitimizes juvenile delinquency. This delinquent subculture may take several forms. The *conflict* gang, engaging often in gratuitous violence, exists in highly disorganized sections of the city where there is no stable adult criminal activity. The *criminal* subculture develops in relatively stable areas where adult crime is organized, extensive, and not violent. The *retreatist* (drug-user) subculture, almost a residual category, consists of those who cannot or will not be meaninglessly violent or use older criminals as models for their own behavior. (They are, in effect, double failures: they have failed to compete in the middle-class pattern, and they have failed to be retained within either the conflict or criminal subcultures.) Generally, the form of delinquency depends on the nature of the neighborhood and the availability of illegitimate opportunities; primarily important here is the existence or nonexistence of adult criminal gangs which have achieved some *modus vivendi* with the noncriminal population. Most juvenile delinquents, according to this theory, do not aspire to the middle class; they merely want to improve their economic lot. This, of course, diverges from the position of Sykes and Matza and of Cohen and Short, who maintain that the delinquent in his subculture eliminates any feelings of guilt by means of certain neutralization techniques (including reaction-formation). Cloward and Ohlin contend that the delinquent has no internalized guilt because it is the larger social order—the indifferent middle class—that is to blame through its failure to provide sufficient legitimate opportunities of success for the lower-class child.

Cultural Transmission

Clifford Shaw and Henry D. McKay[15] *Juvenile Delinquency and Urban Areas,* published in 1942, presents a vast body of data on the ecological distribution of delinquents in many major cities throughout the United States. The evidence consistently demonstrates that the segment of the city which borders on the central business districts (ecological Zone II) had all the characteristics of social disorganization: poor and overcrowded housing, high mortality rates, etc., as well as a disproportionately large amount of juvenile delinquency. The authors propose what has come to be known as the "cultural transmission" theory of delinquency. They suggest that in these disorganized areas there exists a widespread acceptance of non-conventional, illegitimate values, but that these illicit norms compete and conflict with the conventional values, which are still maintained by many in the same area; the illegitimate norms never become dominant, even in the worst neighborhoods (i.e., those of highest delinquency). The deviant-value code of behavior exists because "the groups in the areas of lowest economic status find themselves at a disadvantage in the struggle to achieve the goals idealized in our society. These differences are translated into conduct through the general struggle for those economic symbols which signify a desirable position in the larger social order." Children in these areas of least opportunity are continually aware of the existence and presence of the "successful" criminal; he is known to engage in crime, but he still remains free and displays all the material accoutrements of success—the expensive car, the custom-made suits, the costly girl friend on his arm. Additionally, many youths in those neighborhoods are subjected to considerable pressure from their organized peer-group gangs to engage in occasional illicit activities. In effect, they succumb to delinquency in order to reconcile their idealized status goals—what they hope to get out of life—with the recognizably dim prospect of attaining these goals by noncriminal, legitimate means. The children in these areas are exposed to the "luxury values and success patterns of our culture," and crime is one path (albeit an illicit one) toward obtaining these highly prized goals. Crime is, indeed, their surest path to material success. It tends, accordingly, to become a tradition within these areas where the child is offered one possible means of being successful, of securing the objects symbolic of success in our society. The study demonstrated that in the most disorganized sections of Chicago patterns of high delinquency have been maintained over a 30-year period during which five different ethnic or racial groups (the most recent being, of course, Negroes) have numerically dominated these sections. As each minority group achieved financial success and moved out, the new incoming migrant groups quickly demonstrated high-delinquency patterns; and as they in turn moved out, their delinquency rates dropped.

Walter B. Miller[16] In 1958, Walter B. Miller proposed a systematic explanation of delinquency which is, perhaps, closer to the cultural transmission theory than to Merton and Cohen's anomie theory. Like Shaw and McKay's theory, Miller's theory was based on his own considerable research in delinquency. His major point is that the really important influence on lower-class gang delinquency is not a delinquent subculture but the entire lower-class community, which is in conflict with the middle-class value system. Lower-class culture is a prevalent mode of adaption for unsuccessful migrants, immigrants, and Negroes. It is not highly disorganized,

as is so often inferred, but, perhaps surprisingly, relatively homogeneous and stable. The "focal areas" of the lower class are the
female-based household (often, homes are broken, a paramour is
present, the mother is a breadwinner, and the females form a
matriarchy) and the one-sex peer group (the "emotional haven"
and major area of support for the child [in the middle class, the
family services this function]). The lower-class emphases are on
autonomy, fate, excitement, smartness, toughness, and trouble.
("Trouble is what life gets you into.") In many ways, Miller's
view of lower-class life and the way it relates to delinquency remains
the most persuasive model of delinquency currently available.

Conclusions

One feature common to all the anomic theories of delinquency is
the preoccupation with two major sociological variables: social organization ("gang" delinquencies) and class position (the lower or
working class). When proposing to construct theories of gang behavior, one should be aware of certain problems. First of all, there
is as yet no commonly used definition of a gang nor any general
consensus in the field on what constitutes a gang. The degree of
formal organization necessary, the minimum (and maximum?) number of members required (Can there be a two-person gang?), and
the degree of control that must be exercised over the individual
members of the group are simply not dealt with. All too often, what
is found is an implicit assumption that we all somehow *know* what
a gang is and that there is no need to try to define it. It is also possible to ask what percentage of all juvenile delinquents belong to
gangs or what percentage of *serious* delinquents belong to gangs. If
those belonging to gangs constitute only a relatively small percentage, should we not be concerned with the construction of a
theory of non-gang delinquency? Or is it to be supposed that sub-
stantially the same causative elements operate on gang and non-gang
delinquents? The evidence currently available fails to demonstrate
convincingly that most youthful deviants belong to gangs or that
most delinquencies (serious or not) stem directly from gang life.

The question then becomes, If we can accurately explain gang-delinquent behavior and simultaneously offer an effective action program for its reduction or elimination, how much would the universe of serious delinquents and delinquencies known to public authorities be reduced?

The focus on lower-class delinquency is found in the cultural transmission theories of delinquency as well as the anomic theories. There can be no question that the vast majority of all official delinquents are from the lower class, but is the "lower class" a homogeneous stratum of society? Are the same structural variables operating with equal force on both Negro and white lower class members? Is the Negro lower class sufficiently similar to the white lower class that the variable of race becomes irrelevant or of minor importance? The possibility in each case seems unlikely. Would it, therefore, not be possible that some class-based models are more "correct" for Negroes than for whites or vice versa?

A very strong argument could be made for constructing a theory of *Negro* delinquency and criminality which would be quite different from any possible model of criminal behavior among whites. Such a theory must first of all take take into account the tragic history of the Negro in America. For almost 250 years Negroes were taken forcibly from Africa and brought to a life of slavery. The dehumanizing effect of slave life in America is brilliantly depicted in Stanley M. Elkins' *Slavery* (University of Chicago Press, Chicago, 1959). They were freed only after a brutal and violent civil war, and the reconstruction period saw the legal inferiority of slavery replaced by an almost equally rigid system of social, economic, and political inferiority. It would seem that Walter Miller's belief that the entire lower class exhibits a set of values and a code of behavior sharply at variance with those of the middle class is particularly accurate when applied to the Negro ghetto, which is still segregated from the white world.

The family structure of lower-class Negroes (perhaps 80 to 90 percent of all Negroes are in the lower class) still reflects influences of slavery and reconstruction, where the one enduring bond was between mother and child; the father, even if present, usually exerted minimal influence. However, it would probably be inaccurate to consider a broken home—a home where one or both parents are absent because of death, desertion, or divorce—to be necessarily highly criminogenic; the situation is much more complex. The Negro home, when compared with the average white home, is more likely to be broken; and the family is much more usually a matriarchy, with the mother making the important familial decisions and often being the major breadwinner. At the same time, the Negro family is frequently consanguinal and of an extended nature, which may have beneficent effects. It seems likely that when the father, because of his nonpresence or low evaluation, cannot be an appropriate male model of behavior for a young boy, some other older male in this extended family setting—perhaps a grandfather, uncle, or cousin—becomes the father figure for the boy. Perhaps it is only where the father is not present and his function is not taken over by another that the boy is more likely to tend toward delinquency.

One other remnant of slave days is perhaps important also. The relative position of an ethnic or racial group within the social structure (particularly in large urban centers) may be causally related to deviant behavior. When a group is assigned the lowest status within a society, is considered most inferior, and is continually used as a scapegoat and an object of low regard, its members are not able to project their hostility, frustration, and hatred upon some other lower groups. It is suggested that venting one's prejudice toward a socially inferior nationality or race, whatever its disadvantages (and they are legion), may serve as a substitute for channeling some aspects of hostility in the form of delinquent or criminal behavior. Negroes, now expressing a discontent that has been mounting for centuries, have never been anywhere but at the absolute bottom of the heap, if indeed they have not always been a distinct, separate, and inferior caste. Puerto Ricans have enormous economic, educational, linguistic, and cultural handicaps, even greater than those of the contemporary Negro; they should, therefore, demonstrate a higher delinquency rate than Negroes, but they do not. Perhaps Puerto Ricans, although inferior to Negroes in many socio-economic categories, nevertheless perceive themselves and are perceived by the larger (non-Negro) society as somehow "superior" to the Negro population.[17]

Dilemma

The proper function or role of criminological theory is perhaps the first issue we should deal with. To some, this function is the production of a *true* and complete causal model or explanation of criminal behavior. On the other hand, a theory may represent the best possible "fitting together" of all factors currently known to be associated with delinquency. But should we be primarily concerned with the creation and verification of perfect theories of criminality, or are there not urgent societal needs which might be better served by less ambitious models? The dilemma involves the fact that a theory of criminal behavior ideally must be based on facts and must be true and complete. But a "true and complete" theory implies an enormously difficult goal; while we are taking the time and resources to pursue so ambitious an end, might not the pressing, immediate needs of society be neglected? On the other hand, to attempt to answer those immediate needs while not in possession of a sufficient body of information would seem a necessarily futile undertaking. Is there any way to resolve this?

Let us examine an illustrative case: the history of yellow fever. In the early part of this century medical science came to recognize that epidemic yellow fever is somehow spread by the *Aëdes aegypti* mosquito. As these insects were known to breed in pools of clear water near human habitation, an absolute control of yellow fever was affected by the elimination of places where water collected and stood, as took place in Cuba and later in the Panama Canal Zone. Thus while very little was known about the three factors that must coexist (the causative virus, the functionally active mosquito, and the susceptible human being) and even less was known about the manner in which they interrelate (the mosquito must feed on a man already infected for 3 or 4 days; it draws the virus from his blood, and after an extrinsic incubation period of 10 to 14 days the mosquito is capable of infecting a man susceptible to the disease). It was nevertheless possible to construct an extraordinarily successful program which wiped out the disease. It is perhaps incumbent upon some contemporary sociologists to offer models of delinquency which are capable of being "put to the test" by serving as the theoretical underpinnings for programs aimed at the reduction or prevention of delinquency. The outcome of such programs would to some extent indicate the validity of the particular theory they were based on.

Moreover, we may consider some situations that might arise even after a theory of the causes of crime had somehow been proven true. Such a theory would give all the necessary and sufficient conditions and would accurately describe the interaction among them. But perhaps some causal factors would be, for all practical purposes, unalterable. If an oldest child is more prone to delinquency simply because of his ordinal position, or if certain genetic factors provably predispose a person to crime, what can be done about it? Could legislation be passed restricting family size, or could the government sponsor a vast program of negative eugenics involving sterilization? Are there not, after all, ethical limitations to societal reactions even to a condition as serious as crime? If there were no ethical limitations, we could completely eliminate any possibility of criminal recidivism by executing all convicted offenders or by performing brain surgery which would turn them into vegetables.

There are also practical limitations. Suppose for example, Cloward and Ohlin's theory of differential opportunity became the foundation of an intensive social-work project. In this particular case, the aim would be to maximize lower-class legitimate opportunities for success. The consequences of such a program would be extremely great. What would be required to equalize opportunities among the several classes would be nothing less than a major reconstructing of American society. The Mobilization for Youth program in the lower East Side of New York is in fact based to a considerable extent on the Cloward-Ohlin theory. The social workers involved have permitted (some say even instigated) rent strikes and other types of behavior which have been strongly criticized by "spokesmen" for the middle class. Some theories, it would seem, are dangerous in that they are far too threatening to conventional society: the prices they hold that must be paid to reduce delinquency are perhaps too high. If school dropouts *cause* delinquency, we can keep people in school longer; if neurosis underlies much deviant behavior, we can supply more psychiatric aid. But if we must massively alter our entire way of life, what are we to do?

LAW ENFORCEMENT IN THE UNITED STATES

The past century has witnessed profound, even revolutionary changes in Western civilization. Among the most important of these has been a rapid urbanization, with its resultant emphasis on superficial, secondary-group types of social relationships. In addition, there has been a decline in previously effective means of informal social control such as the family and the church. The creation and growth of formal agencies of law enforcement inevitably resulted. These organizations and their personnel have been granted special police power to detain, search, interrogate, and arrest persons suspected of having committed criminal actions. Modern police forces continue some of their historical practices of social control, but the scope and nature of their operations are vastly different today.

The primary function of the police is to prevent the commission of all crime; failing this ideal goal, they are to detect and report all lawlessness, apprehend probable offenders, and secure all relevant evidence which might lead to the conviction of suspects. Unhappily, the police are also burdened with many ancillary tasks, few of them closely related to law enforcement; these nevertheless consume a large proportion of the limited police resources available.

Virtually every autonomous governmental jurisdiction in the United States has its own police force; these forces range from a sheriff and his deputies in rural areas to large, extremely complex bureaucracies in metropolitan communities. There are at least 40,000 separate law-enforcement agencies in the United States today. For 3,664 cities with a total population of over 104,000,000 in 1963, the *Uniform Crime Reports* shows a total of 202,000 police officers, or an average of about 2 policemen per 1,000 inhabitants. The *police ratio* is the number of policemen per 1,000 residents. On the basis of these figures, of the 29 largest cities in the United States, Washington, D.C. had the highest police ratio: 4.1. (New York and Boston were close behind with 3.9.) San Antonio had the lowest: 1.2. Generally, the larger the city is, the higher its ratio is; cities with populations over 250,000 averaged 2.7, whereas the smallest cities (populations of 10,000 and under) averaged only 1.4.

In addition to the local, state, and rural police agencies, there are of course Federal law-enforcement activities, including the Secret Service, Bureau of Narcotics, Coast Guard, and Immigration Service under the Treasury Department. The Internal Revenue Service, America's great *bête noire*, has both intelligence units, which investigate cases of income tax fraud and evasion, and customs units. The Post Office Department is concerned with various postal offenses—legitimately in its actions against using the mail to defraud, and more controversially in its quasi-legal actions against sending obscene material through the mail. Without question, the most highly publicized and best-regarded of all governmental police agencies is the Federal Bureau of Investigation. The F.B.I. was organized in 1908 and had a rather unsavory early history, particularly after World War I; it rose to major importance after being reorganized in 1924 by its current director, J. Edgar Hoover. The Bureau investigates bankruptcy frauds, violations of antitrust laws, certain forms of bribery, crimes on the high seas and on Indian reservations, espionage, violation of the Federal kidnapping act, interstate transportation of stolen property (including automobiles), robbery of national and Federal Reserve

Systems banks, and violations of the Mann Act, or White Slave Traffic Act (which prohibits the interstate transportation of females for "immoral purposes"). Additionally, the Bureau maintains a well-regarded crime laboratory which utilizes all the most recent criminalistic techniques and devices. (Despite popular belief, however, the crime laboratory cannot determine from a single hair found on the scene of the crime how many children the criminal had, how many he wants to have, and whether he had hog jowls, or whether he had had sole Veronique for lunch a week before.)[1]

Law-enforcement authorities are granted a monopoly of the legitimate use of force within their political jurisdictions, and this power often extends to matters of life and death. Thus when all other means of preventing the escape of a felon have failed, the policeman is expected to kill the fleeing offender. This is both *justified* under the law and occupationally *required* of the policeman. In view of this power, and in addition the great latitude of permissible violence, the singular importance of the work they do, and the difficulty and danger commonly recognized as being an integral part of their job, it is perhaps surprising that the dominant sociological fact about police work in the United States today is the low regard in which policemen are held by the public. For example, a national survey was conducted by the National Opinion and Research Center in 1947 under Cecil C. North and Paul K. Hatt on the prestige ranking of 90 occupations. The policeman was ranked fifty-fourth—equal in status to railroad conductors and playground directors, and below undertakers and traveling salesmen.[2] This low valuation of law-enforcement personnel is probably a uniquely American phenomenon and a direct consequence of a general belief that the police are basically inefficient, corrupt, and brutal.

Inefficiency

Incompetence is the basis for much public antipathy toward the police. The most extensive national survey of police operations and efficiency in the United States, carried out in 1930 by the Wickersham Commission, concluded that the great majority of policemen were not suited by temperament, training, or education for their positions.[3] Belief in the inadequacy of the policeman has not slackened to the present day, despite the many improvements that have taken place in the quality of the police and police organizations over the past several decades. Higher minimum educational requirements, increased civil service jurisdiction resulting in greater job security, occupational advancement based primarily on competitive examinations, and extended and vastly improved police training facilities have produced probably the best-qualified and most efficient police forces in our history.

Increased reliance on contemporary criminalistic techniques and devices has proved more and more important in improving the efficiency of many law-enforcement agencies. The most publicized of these is the polygraph, or lie detector, which is an elaborate instrument recording changes in blood pressure, pulse, respiration, psychogalvanic skin reflex and, optionally, muscular activity.

In a pretest interview, the subject is told what the questioning is about and exactly what questions he will be asked. He is advised that if he lies, this will be clearly indicated by the machine. Two tests are commonly given. The "control-question" test devotes about half its questions to irrelevant items dealing with known facts, such as: Did you eat breakfast today? Are you a licensed driver? The remaining five or six questions are relevant to the offense for which the subject is being tested. As the subject answers the questions "yes" or "no," his responses are precisely marked on a moving chart that records and measures physiological changes. When this part of the test (seldom taking more than 5 minutes) is over, a second examination is given in which the subject picks out one card from a pile of seven, shows it to the examiner, and is then shown one card at a time and is instructed to answer "no" when asked, for each card, whether it is the one he had picked. In one instance, of course, he is forced to give false information. This is to allow measurement of his "normal reaction" while lying. He is then shown how his lie is indicated on the chart. Then the first test is repeated, with the same questions in the same order. If the subject's "lying reaction" is measureably greater on the relevant than the irrelevant questions, it is claimed that he is probably guilty.

In its initial stages, the "peak-of-tension" test is similar to the other in that the subject is told generally about the offense for which he is being questioned; but in this test he is not given any details about the crime. Each of the questions relates to a single item involved in the crime, an item about which only the criminal would have any knowledge. For example, a list of objects in approximately the same category as a key "clue" could be drawn up, and the subject would be asked if he knows anything about a brass key, a zipper, a brown comb (the key item), a gray coat button, etc.[4]

Based on the idea that an individual cannot control all the physiological concomitants of lying, the tests attempt to maximize the pressures that produce these physiological changes. The tests are not perfect, however. An examiner's inexperience or bias, badly constructed questions, or a subject who is extremely tense, very fatigued, psychopathic, or psychotic will make the results of a test questionable. Results of polygraph tests are not yet admissible in our courts of law; but the police persist in the use of the polygraph, believing that it can confirm or refute their suspicions about a subject's guilt, aid them in their criminal investigations, and occasionally cause a criminal to confess to his crime.

Corruption

It is an unfortunate fact of contemporary life that a few police officers are bribed, particularly in those jurisdictions where illicit alliances already exist between important political personages and professional criminal organizations. It was not so many years ago that the open and blatant corruption of the highest echelons of metropolitan police forces was a matter of common knowledge, occasioning no violent public reaction because it was thought to be almost inevitable. In 1930, it was widely circulated in New York City that one could purchase a sergeantcy or higher rank on the local police force; *The New York Times* reported that police captaincies were selling for $5,000 or more, depending on where the "applicant" wanted to be assigned. In 1951 the Kefauver Committee concluded that police dishonesty was still significant; the committee estimated, for example, that monthly "payoffs" amounted to over

$150,000 for Philadelphia alone.[5] Corruption, however, has become less open, less extensive, and subject to very heavy criticism. Whenever bribery or, even worse, police criminality is uncovered, it becomes a major scandal and a matter of disgrace and embarrassment to the entire department.[6] But with probably a quarter of a million policemen in the country, many of whom are continually being tempted by offers of bribes, it is perhaps only to be expected that some will succumb to temptation. Would an equal number of higher-status businessmen be better able to resist? It is paradoxical that society seems to demand so high a standard of moral behavior from policemen when it pays them poorly and holds them in low esteem.

Illegality

Actual police criminality, such as bribery, burglary, and robbery, falls into the category of corruption. Lawless behavior by the police, however, includes additional and far more extensive illegal acts. Of these, the best known are police actions which go beyond the letter and spirit of the law and effectively deny constitutionally guaranteed individual civil liberties. These acts of police "brutality" (the inclusive term most commonly used) arouse considerable hostility and represent the most important factor fostering and reinforcing the low valuation placed on law-enforcement agencies today. There is another very extensive illegality, however, which is less well known: the police frequently fail to perform all of their legally prescribed functions. They deliberately fail to detect or record all crime they are aware of, and they avoid arresting all appropriate suspects. This underreporting and underarresting is clearly illegal, as it involves the usurpation of judicial power by law-enforcement personnel. Although provoking little societal reaction, this failure to invoke arrest procedure enormously affects our knowledge of the extent of criminal behavior in the United States.

Discretion in Reporting and Arrest A fundamental tenet of law enforcement in this country is that the police, ideally, are to detect and record *all* crimes and arrest *all* probable offenders. Presumably the police are not expected to differentiate between a traffic violator and a mass murderer; both are criminals who should be arrested and upon conviction should receive an appropriate punishment from the authorized judicial authorities.

In reality, an occasional police force will deliberately underreport the number of crimes brought to its attention in order to produce a deceptively high clearance rate and thereby appease a critical public. New York City's crime records control, by the late 1940's, was marked by such laxity and inaccuracy that the data were excluded by the Federal Bureau of Investigation from the *Uniform Crime Reports*. Accordingly, in October of 1950, the city instituted a new, much stricter system of recording procedures; consequently, the recorded number of certain types of crime rose sharply. The number of burglaries recorded by the police had not been above 282 for any month from 1947 through September, 1950. For the following 12 months, the lowest monthly burglary figure was 1,185. For larceny the monthly figure from 1947 through September, 1950, was always under 750, whereas for October, 1950 to September, 1951, it was in every case above 2,600.[7]

Such large-scale falsification of statistics of major crimes can be prevented by adequate record control, but little can be done about the discretionary and sometimes arbitrary decisions that policemen make daily when they arrest in one instance and not in another, similar instance. Prof. Wayne La Fave, after close examination, suggests that the dominant characteristics of decisions not to arrest are (1) that they involve crimes of low visibility, i.e., offenses not likely to become known to the public, and (2) that the means of "challenging" this practice are extremely limited.[8] He notes several circumstances in which this exercise of discretion may take place. First the police may decide not to arrest if they believe the legislature does not really want the relevant laws enforced. If a statute dealing with a particular crime is unclear, perhaps poorly drafted, its ambiguity may cast doubt on the policeman's lawful right to arrest someone for that crime without a warrant. Similarly, if a law is thought to have been enacted primarily to permit investigation rather than arrest and punishment—e.g., some vagrancy statutes—

the police may fail to record the crime or arrest the offender. Other crimes may be overlooked if they remain crimes only because of legislative inertia (e.g., offenses covered by obsolescent "blue laws") or if they manifest a legislative desire to have the substantive law enunciate community ideals rather than coerce obedience. Thus adultery laws remain unenforced because of a generally permissive view toward adultery, and yet the statutes prohibiting adultery continue in existence because it is assumed they help preserve a "high moral tone."

Another condition influential in failure to arrest concerns the most efficient disposition and use of scarce police resources. For trivial offenses (such as traffic violations) a warning may be thought sufficient. Often, no official action will be taken if some prohibited behavior is considered normal and usual for a particular subgroup in the community, for example, nonviolent sex offenses among Negroes. Similarly, if the victim is reluctant to prosecute, being related to the criminal or interested only in restitution or personal revenge, experience has shown that the offense is not likely to result in conviction. The rationale in such instances is that law-enforcement facilities are more effectively utilized elsewhere.

The police may also fail to arrest if they believe the punishment is inappropriate or ineffective (e.g., in the case of chronic skid-row alcoholics who are neither aided nor deterred by any available penalty) or if the public is strongly opposed to the enforcement of a particular law, as law-enforcement agencies are often subject to popular control. If an arrest will harm the victim (as in some rape cases) or cause greater pain to the criminal than the law intended, or if an arrest would vitally disrupt police activities (as in the apprehension and "taking out of action" of a valuable police informer who has committed a trivial offense), it is likely arrest procedure will not be invoked.

Professor La Fave contends, however, that the reverse sometimes occurs: the police will on occasion arrest in a specific case despite a policy of not usually enforcing the criminal statute involved. Reasons for this would include coercing respect for a police officer; maintaining public belief in the full enforcement of the law (as when a crime is blatant and known to many); aiding in the investigation of other, more serious offenses; punishing a chronic offender; and reducing cases which place a continual strain upon insufficient police resources (as when one or both parties to a series of family squabbles which frequently involve the police are finally arrested).

Brutality The concept of police brutality is most meaningful when applied to all instances in which the police exceed their legal prerogatives. Such instances range from illegal detentions and "friskings" on the street to unlawful violence and the physical and psychological mistreatment of suspects. It must be kept in mind that there are real and increasingly precise constitutional limits to police powers of arrest and interrogation. Indeed, these limitations are of such proportions that many policemen, perhaps unaware of the paradox involved, feel they must go beyond these restrictions in order to fulfill their role properly. They point out that if they operated precisely within the law, the proportion of crimes known to the police which are cleared by arrest would certainly decrease greatly.

The law of arrest, for example, varies with whether or not a warrant is secured. In obtaining a warrant, a full statement concerning the complaint must be given to the issuing agency. The warrant is then granted for an indefinite period and is "fair on its face" when it gives the name or complete physical description, or both, of the offender. (The description must be so complete and accurate that a policeman can arrest the right suspect on the basis of it alone.) To arrest without a warrant for a felony, generally the policeman must "know" that a felony has been committed and have "reasonable grounds" for supposing that the suspect is the offender. The police believe that securing a warrant is a slow and cumbersome process which frequently permits the criminal to escape. Similarly, they believe that the effectiveness of the police is unfairly limited by strict adherence to the "reasonable grounds" provisions for arrests without a warrant. A study of Philadelphia police practices in 1952 found that 97 percent of all arrests were without warrants, the police contending that getting a warrant would result in the offender's being forewarned and escaping; despite the illegality of some arrests without warrants, they were an effective means of getting offenders into police custody.[9] Illegal arrests included those which were made on a basis of radio messages giving only the address of the crime and no description of the offender, and arrests for "suspicious circumstances" (an example of the latter would be the arrest of a Negro carrying a suitcase in a white area). Other police practices included illegal searches, "friskings," and detentions for interrogations.

It is important to recognize that illegal police action often produces results which the general public applauds. One small section of West Philadelphia had an extremely high crime rate in 1942, which the police felt was due to the operation of two poolrooms and one bar in the area. One day they rounded up indiscriminately over 300 persons in the three establishments. After releasing those who were regularly employed, they found in the possession of the rest enough guns and knives to fill several baskets. Additionally, 12 persons wanted for major crimes were seized; and the crime rate in the neighborhood during the next two months dropped 80 percent for serious offenses and 50 percent for all crimes.[10] But in the accomplishment of these ends over 250 people were gratuitously and illegally arrested and deprived of fundamental constitutional guarantees.

Why the police should engage in illegal acts of violence was the problem Professor William Westley undertook to examine.[11] He concluded that the police both accept and morally justify the use of violence and that this justification is closely related to their low occupational status. A large proportion of the American population react to the police with undisguised hostility, and some policemen in turn react to this by attempting to *coerce* respect if they can gain respect only by coercion. The use of violence by the police is both an occupational prerogative and often a legal necessity. (From 1960 through 1963, for example, 163 police officers were killed in the line of duty by felons and 16,793 were assaulted.)[12] It is Westley's belief that "from experience in the pursuit of their legally prescribed duties, police develop a justification for the use of violence. They come to see it as good, as useful and as their own." The very essence of good police work is not the daily investigations, arrests, and interrogations of which most people are unaware; rather it is the apprehension and conviction of the *felon* (particularly for a highly publicized offense). A "good pinch" is one that is politically clear, aids in career advancement and, most importantly, justifies the continued existence of the police to a basically unsympathetic public. Violence, accordingly, comes to be a legitimate means for obtaining evidence which might result in the conviction of a felon. When a number of policemen were asked by Westley when they thought a policeman is justified in "roughing up" someone, seven situations were mentioned; but of these only two ("when it was impossible to avoid" and "to make an arrest") were legally permissible instances. The other (illegal) circumstances included displays of disrespect for police; instances where it is necessary to "get information"; and instances where the arrested person is a "hardened" criminal, is "known to be guilty," or is a sex offender.

After decades of indifference to the systematic invasion of individual civil liberties by law-enforcement agencies, the United States Supreme Court, in a series of recent decisions, has set rigid guidelines as to what constitutes illegal police practices and the procedural consequences of such behavior. In *Mapp v. Ohio* (1961) the Court found that evidence obtained during an illegal search or seizure was thenceforth inadmissible in *both* state and Federal courts. (Wiretapping, apparently, is not subsumed under the search and seizure provisions of the Fourth Amendment, and therefore it seems that evidence obtained by wiretapping may be admissible in court.) The *Escobedo* decision in 1964 stated that the suspect has a constitutional right to counsel *when arrested* and that he must be advised of his right to remain silent. The *McNabb-Mallory* rule (of 1943 and 1957) held that confessions were not acceptable if made during illegal detention, which includes the failure to bring the suspect to a magistrate promptly. The rule applies only to Federal cases, but it has had a considerable effect in discouraging both illegal arrests and coerced confessions.[13]

Dilemma

The discretionary nonenforcement of the criminal law, involving, as it usually does, minor crimes of low visibility, does not appreciably affect the precarious interaction between the police and the public. On the other hand, to demonstrate their indispensability and appease a hostile public, the police often exceed their legal prerogatives to make an "important" arrest or solve a highly publicized crime. And for years, law-enforcement agencies have ignored fundamental individual civil rights with relative impunity. Such actions have had a great effect on the relationship between the public and the police. Recent Supreme Court decisions have now taken a firm position confirming the constitutional guarantees for the protection of accused persons. The Court has, however, been criticized for this by some who feel that as a result of these decisions too many actual criminals will be freed. It is believed by some that our best protection against crime would be an extension of police power and a limitation of the rights of suspects. These attacks are often specious, intemperate, and, upon close examination, extraordinarily unpersuasive.

The dilemma is simply that we cannot ensure perfect protection for the innocent from arrest and at the same time guarantee that the guilty will always be detected and arrested. A system set up with conviction of the guilty as its overriding concern will doubtless punish some innocent suspects; a system most concerned with the rights of suspects will be likely to find that some genuine offenders slip from its grasp. Each alternative entails some undesirable results. The current controversy over the matter reflects not only the clash of philosophies but the practical matter of balancing the protection of suspects and the protection of society.

There are several possible resolutions of the conflict between police power and civil liberties. None is a permanent solution, and none is without considerable drawbacks. First, the police could continue to operate in the same way as they have in the past, illegally exceeding newly defined restrictions on search, seizure, arrest, and interrogation. They could justify their behavior by stating that these practices are effective and that most convictions based to some extent on such illegalities, are not, as a matter of fact, carried to appellate courts, where they might be reversed. This course of action would create a new gray area of police operations. The courts and the public would wink at certain practices, convinced that they produce the desired results of higher clearance rates and more convictions, while at the same time civil rights would theoretically remain intact. Obviously, any such solution simply avoids the central problem of reconciling the appropriate protection of society and the appropriate safeguards for the rights of any individual member of the society. It amounts to simply closing our eyes in the hope that the problem will disappear.

Second, new legislation could be passed, perhaps even new constitutional amendments, which would legitimize previously illegal law-enforcement practices. We could even go beyond this and extend unprecedented power to the police in investigation, detention, stop-and-frisk, arrest, and interrogation. Possibly the Supreme Court could be persuaded to reverse its previous decisions in this area, and to uphold this increase in the authorized range of police power by novel reinterpretations. Support for this approach is based on the belief that society is best protected by maximizing permissible police practices to combat crime and by a willingness to accept the cost of this policy: decreased constitutional safeguards not only for the criminal suspect but for every member of the society. It is here argued that crime is rising and the increase is *primarily* due to court restrictions on the power of the police. We must therefore unshackle the police, it is held, so that they may more adequately perform their duties; this would also raise their morale, which has sagged badly in the face of the recent court decisions.

Finally, the police could be forced to accept their present position, however reluctantly, as being relatively fixed, with any illegality on their part resulting in the release of the offender. They would simply have to learn to live and operate within these new restrictions. There would be no gray area, no accommodations, and no legislative extension of their law-enforcement powers. For such a solution to operate efficiently, it would be necessary for officers to be trained to know precisely what they may or may not legally do. Those who argue for this approach contend that it is difficult to prove that crime rates are increasing; and that even if an increase were demonstrable, it is unlikely that it would be related to Supreme Court decisions. Further, it is argued that the police, even under these new restrictions, are not unreasonably limited in the scope of their activity. Society is best protected by improving the quality, efficiency, competence, and training of police officers. Greater reliance on scientific methods of crime detection and a campaign to reduce general hostility to the police should also be beneficial. It is argued that we must maintain the current proscription of involuntary confessions, failure to arraign a suspect promptly, and deprivation of advice of counsel; some even suggest that perhaps the courts should go beyond their recent holdings in their efforts to safeguard individual liberties. As a consequence of this policy, however, we would have to anticipate that police forces might be occasionally demoralized and confused, might feel that their activities have been almost fatally hampered, and might in consequence adopt a halfhearted approach to law enforcement. Also, without doubt, this policy would result in fewer arrests and fewer convictions than either of the other possible solutions. But these drawbacks might be more bearable than the loss of those basic rights that are the quintessence of the American way of life.[14]

FROM CRIME TO CRIMINAL:

the administration of criminal justice

As has been made clear previously, our primary source of information on the extent and differentials of crime in the United States is reporting by law-enforcement agencies. The *Uniform Crime Reports*, with minor reservations, may be considered to represent crimes which come to the attention of the police and which the police decide to incorporate in their statistical records. On the average, about two-thirds of all crimes known to the police are not cleared by arrest, although of course the clearance rate varies considerably by offense. When a suspect is arrested, the first necessary step has been taken in a process which may finally result in his being designated a criminal—our basic unit of concern. It must be kept in mind that in our system of jurisprudence, the accused is considered innocent until proven guilty beyond a reasonable shadow of doubt in a court of law.

In any analysis of the operation of criminal procedure in the United States, it is important, at the outset, to indicate that there is considerable variation in specific details from one state to another and even from one county to another. Nevertheless, the major procedural features discussed in this chapter are generally true for the country as a whole.[1]

Police Detention

After a suspect is detained and arrested by the police, he is brought to some place of detention, where he is interrogated. Then, within a "short time," it is required that he *should* be brought before an inferior court (a magistrate's court or a justice of the peace) for a preliminary examination. The American Civil Liberties Union made a study of illegal detention by the police in Chicago and concluded that 50 percent of a sample of prisoners produced in Felony Court were held without "booking," i.e., the entering of formal charges and the setting of bail at the police station, for over 17 hours from the time they were arrested. Moreover, this figure did *not* take into account the additional period of detention after booking and before a magistrate's hearing. For an additional 30 percent of all defendants, it was impossible to determine their period of detention because the police had failed to complete their arrest slips properly. Thus the files showed that only 20 percent of those accused of crimes were booked in less than 17 hours.[2]

The Magistrate

The magistrate has "summary jurisdiction"; that is, he determines guilt or innocence and can sentence, within very strict limits, for minor, nonindictable offenses. Though of a petty nature, these offenses constitute the bulk of all criminal charges; and Puttkammer suggests that "they are conceivably of more social significance than the major crimes."[3] For more serious, indictable offenses, the magistrate performs a very different role: he holds a "preliminary hearing" in which he determines whether the evidence presented is sufficient to warrant holding the suspect for further action, that is, whether the state has made a prima-facie case. He does not solicit new evidence, but on the basis of only what he is told by all parties he will either hold or release the suspect. This hearing, therefore, is simultaneously a prosecuting device and an instrument for the protection of the accused.

Bail or Jail[4]

Another function of the minor judiciary is the setting of bail after it has been decided there is sufficient cause to bind the accused over to the grand jury. The purpose of bail is simply to guarantee the presence of the defendant at the trial and at the same time permit him to avoid the debilitating experience of being jailed. The Eighth Amendment of the Constitution provides that "excessive" bail should not be required. However, what constitutes "reasonable" bail is determined by the magistrate. The defendant, if he can, may offer as security something of value equal to the amount of the bail. "Neither the requirement for bail nor pre-trial detention in default of bail is a punitive device."[5] The advantages of bail are obvious: the accused avoids institutionalization, he is free to maintain himself and his family until the trial, and there is no cost to the state of maintaining him or his family while he is in jail. Unhappily the amount of bail required is frequently unrelated to the likelihood that the accused will be present at his trial, but is rather a function of the seriousness of the charge. If the accused cannot by himself raise bail, he may secure the services of a professional bail bondsman who, in effect, lends him money or some property to cover the bail. Regardless of the outcome of this case—whether the accused is convicted or acquitted—he must still pay the bail bondsman for the loan. It follows that the poor defendant is likely to incur unrecoverable costs, as he probably will not have sufficient financial resources to provide for his own bail and will need the services of the bail bondsman.

An investigation of the administration of bail in Philadelphia in 1953 and New York City in 1957 came to the following conclusions: (1) Many defendants could not furnish even nominal amounts of bail. (2) As bail exceeded $1,000, pretrial releases dropped sharply. (3) Bail was set so high for serious felonies that most defendants were not released. (4) *Ten to twenty percent of those not released on bail were not subsequently convicted of any crime.* (5) Defendants who had been jailed did have a higher conviction rate and received more severe penalties.[6] A more recent study of the Manhattan Magistrate Felony Court for October, 1961, to September, 1962, showed that 36 percent of those who had been jailed were later convicted without institutionalization or were acquitted.[7]

The Manhattan Bail Project, begun in 1961, is based on the hypothesis that detention reduces the prospects of rehabilitation of the accused, particularly for first offenders.[8] It contended that a significant number of indigent defendants, who cannot raise bail, might successfully be released on parole pending trial. On a basis of five criteria—mobility, employment record, family residence in New York City, previous criminal record, and length of residence in New York City—the Project recommended, to the Court of Quarter Session, 363 persons for parole. The Court agreed in 215 of the cases, and, with some subsequent paroles, 250 were examined from October, 1961, through 1962. It was found that only 3 (less than 2 percent) had jumped parole; and, strikingly, this rate of parole jumping was much *lower* than the rate of bail jumping (which was over 7 percent).[9]

If the offense is nonbailable (e.g., a capital crime) or the defendant cannot raise bail or be released on parole, he will be kept in a detention institution, usually a jail of one type or another. In 1960, 23,811 persons accused of Federal offenses were held in custody pending trial; their average period of detention was 25.3 days. In 1963, Federal detainees, spending 600,000 jail days in local prisons, cost the Federal government $2,000,000. Detainees in Philadelphia alone in 1964 represented a cost of $1,300,000.[10] Jails, unlike penal institutions, house both persons awaiting trial (and still innocent under the law) and some prisoners, usually those serving short terms. One of the paradoxes of American penology is that substantial populations of people who are only accused of having committed crimes are kept in jails which by any objective standard are almost always worse than the prisons which house only convicts. Survey after survey has found that most jails in this country are fire hazards, dirty, insecure, lax in discipline, and lacking in educational and recreational facilities. A more extensive and rational

use of bail, such as the plan suggested by the Manhattan Bail
Project, would certainly reduce the number of instances when the
punishment of being jailed is inflicted on noncriminals.

The Prosecuting Attorney

The most important person in the entire criminal procedure is the
prosecuting attorney or district attorney. His powers are enormous
both in fact and in law. He may decide not to prosecute a case
(enter a nolle prosequi), and in many jurisdictions he may do this
without the consent of the court. (If a case is nol-prossed after the
trial begins, the effect is identical to that of a court rendering of
not guilty; the accused cannot again be charged with the same
offense in the same jurisdiction, as this would constitute former
[double] jeopardy.) The district attorney may submit the case to the
grand jury for an indictment or, in many instances, bypass the grand
jury by use of a bill of information. He may, legally and properly,
bargain with the defense on what the final charge will be, and he
may prevent prosecution by granting immunity to someone turning
state's evidence. In sum, "there are no important limitations on the
prosecuting attorney's power to terminate a case."[11]

The Grand Jury

The function of the grand jury, relevant to our purpose, is the investigation of criminal charges to decide if the defendant should
be brought to trial; the grand jury does not pass on disputed facts
or determine guilt or innocence. It therefore hears only testimony
presented by the prosecution, the accused having no legal right to be
heard at this point, and on the basis of this evidence concludes
whether or not there is probable cause to believe the suspect guilty.
The role of the grand jury duplicates almost exactly that of the
magistrate; but this duplication is an additional procedural safeguard for the accused, for if either the magistrate or the grand jury
is not convinced that the suspect is the probable offender, he will
be released.

If the grand jury is not persuaded by the prosecution's evidence, it can "ignore" the charge. If, on the other hand, the jury decides that a prima-facie case has been made, a true bill of indictment will be returned. A bill of indictment is a statement of all necessary facts charged against the accused and his asserted offense. If there is any "substantial" error in the indictment requiring any assumption, inference, or interpretation, no matter how slight it may seem —if, in effect, the indictment is not "full and precise"—the appellate court will probably reverse the verdict of the trial court. Thus it has happened that verdicts of guilty were overturned because the bills of indictment contained such errors as the following: (1) A man was charged with stealing a Smith and Weston gun. (It should have been "Smith and Wesson.") (2) Another defendent was accused of having stolen $100 lawful money. (Correctly, "$100 lawful *United States* money.") (3) The phrase used was "against the peace and dignity of state." (The word *the* was omitted.) Puttkammer mentions a reversal where the indictment said that the defendent killed Viola Hughes but did not state that Viola Hughes was a human being, and another where the indictment said that the death was instantaneous, but did not specifically say that the death occurred within a year and a day from the time of the shooting. Perhaps the most incredible case of all was a verdict that was reversed because the indictment said that the killing took place on July 15, 1855, forcing the court and jury to assume that the proper date was July 15, 1855 A.D.!

Arraignment and Plea

At the arraignment the prosecuting attorney formally reads in court the bill of indictment which recites the specific charges lodged against the defendant by the state. The defendant, making his first appearance in a court of record, is asked how he pleads to the charges. The district attorney is legally empowered to bargain with the defendant and his counsel; he may accept a plea of guilty to the indictment charge and promise leniency in return, or he may accept a plea of guilty to some lesser charge. The prosecutor might agree to accept a plea of guilty of a lesser charge if he considers his case weak, if he feels that the potential penalties are too severe for the actual offense, or if he wants to be absolutely certain the defendant will be imprisoned (since he could never be sure what the jury would decide). One study of 97 convicted felons found that 55 of them had engaged in some bargaining with the district attorney: 11 pleaded guilty to a lesser charge than that contained in the indictment; 25 entered a plea of guilty to the indictment charge after the district attorney had said that he would try to get them a light sentence (probation or something less than the maximum sentence); 12 bargained for a concurrent sentence (several charges included together, with their sentences operating concurrently); and 7 pleaded guilty to the major offense in exchange for the dismissal of several lesser charges.[12] The district attorney is not limitless in his power; he may only recommend mercy and a reduced penalty to a sentencing judge, who may or may not follow his advice. In practice, it quickly becomes apparent to defense lawyers which prosecuting attorneys keep their promises and which do not; and those who do not soon find few cases in which the defense will bargain.

The Defense Counsel

Until very recently, if the defendant could not afford counsel, particularly in cases that did not involve felonies, he was not *necessarily* assigned counsel by the court. In *Gideon v. Wainwright* (1963) the United States Supreme Court said that under the Fourteenth Amendment, poverty alone should not deprive a defendant in a criminal case of the right of counsel.[13] It must be admitted that court-assigned attorneys do not inspire great confidence; they are often recent law school graduates or less talented lawyers who survive primarily by engaging in such marginal enterprises. To counteract this, in recent years there arose the idea of a "public defender" who would be paid by the county (or in some instances a charitable agency) to defend those who cannot afford counsel. Public defenders operate in 38 cities or counties, and the general evaluation is that they have been quite successful, as compared with court-assigned counsel, in protecting their clients.

The Judge

Of his major functions, the judge is usually well equipped to preside over the trial; to supervise the selection of the jury; to enforce rules of evidence; to rule on various motions; and to "charge" the jury, i.e., to summarize the salient points of the case to the jury, reviewing the crime and the evidence, telling the jurors how to analyze the evidence, and telling them what verdicts they may return. He is less capable, however, in sentencing, for he has little basis other than his own unique experiences for deciding what is the most appropriate punishment. Nevertheless, within statutory limits he sentences the offender, determines whether or not to grant probation and sets the terms of probation, and may even select an appropriate penal institution. Whether such irrelevant factors as the race of the offender or the victim or both enter into the sentencing of the criminal is still somewhat contentious. When only the race of the offender is examined, differences that may exist do not seem to be significant; however, when the race of the criminal and the race of the victim are both examined, systematic disparities appear, particularly for crimes of violence against the person. Of all homicides in Richmond, Virginia, from 1930 to 1939, 6 percent of the Negro-Negro killings (killings involving a Negro offender and a Negro victim) resulted in life imprisonment or a death sentence, whereas 100 percent of Negro-white killings, 27 percent of white-white killings; and no white-Negro killings produced the same penalties.[14] In 10 counties of North Carolina from 1930 to 1940, 19 of 41 Negro-white killings, 14 of 101 white-white killings, 16 of 372 Negro-Negro killings, and none of 11 white-Negro killings resulted in a life term or a death sentence.[15] Turner's studies of various offenses committed in Forrest County, Mississippi, during the years 1935 to 1939 and 1947 to 1951 revealed, almost without exception, this same pattern of comparatively heavy sentences for Negro-white offenses and light sentences for white Negro crimes.[16] A recent analysis of sentencing differentials in Philadelphia concluded that any racial variations in sentencing were due to the different patterns of crimes the two racial groups engaged in; but this study dealt primarily with nonviolent crimes; Green found that while Negro-Negro crimes usually brought the least penalty, there were no significant differences between sentences for white-white offenders and those for Negro-white offenders.[17]

The Jury

Although the jury is not a necessary element to a trial, as in most jurisdictions the defendant may elect to have a bench trial, the jury continues to be used in a large proportion of all court cases.

A jury, theoretically, is chosen at random from a panel of qualified prospective jurors. Persons may be excused from jury service for various reasons; e.g., lawyers, physicians, and convicts are excused in Pennsylvania. Additionally, prospective jurors may be challenged for "cause" (they may be accused of being biased, related to the defendant or victim, or in some other way lacking the proper qualifications for reaching an objective and fair verdict) or challenged peremptorily. Peremptory challenges permit the arbitrary elimination of a limited number during the *voir dire*. A deliberate and systematic exclusion of any class of people on the basis of social or economic distinction, however, is a denial of "due process of law" (Fifth and Fourteenth Amendments), "equal protection under the law" (Fourteenth Amendment), and the guarantee of a fair trial (Sixth Amendment). The majority of judicial decisions in this area have dealt with the exclusion of Negroes from grand and trial (petit) juries; from *Strauder v. West Virginia* in 1880 to the present, the Supreme Court has consistently ruled against the state whenever the exclusion was provably discriminatory because of race. A study by S. S. Ulmer of how the United States Supreme Court ruled on 13 cases of racial exclusion brought before it between 1935 (*Norris v. Alabama*) and 1958 (*Eubank v. Louisiana*) concluded that when Negroes were totally excluded from jury service the Court always found that this violated the Fourteenth Amendment if Negroes were a substantial percentage of the local population (at least 7.2 percent) and if the exclusion had existed for an appreciable period of time (at least 16 years). Ulmer believed that cases where there was only partial absence of Negroes were also

reversed if the racial composition of the jurors differed to a statistically significant degree from that of the general population.[18]

The Trial

In a criminal trial operating within an Anglo-Saxon system of
jurisprudence, the defendant is entitled to various procedural safeguards subsumed under "due process of law." This includes, among
other things, the right to be present at every session of the trial,
the presumption of innocence until guilt is proven beyond a reasonable doubt, and the right to refuse to testify (the jury is instructed
that it must not take such a refusal into account in arriving at a
verdict). Most information presented during a trial is evidence of a
direct or circumstantial nature or testimony by selected "experts."
Unfortunately, many witnesses are reluctant to testify because of
indifference or fear, or because they will lose income by being
away from their jobs. There is, additionally, the continuing problem
of errors in testimony. It might prove instructive to examine Felix
Frankfurter's analysis of the testimony of Mary E. Splaine, one of
the key prosecution witnesses in the most fascinating and tragic
criminal trial of our century, the Sacco-Vanzetti case:

> "Splaine, viewing the scene from a distance of from 60 to 80 feet, saw
> a man previously unknown to her, in a car traveling at a rate of from
> 15 to 18 miles per hour; she saw him only from a distance of about 30
> feet, that is to say for one and a half to three seconds; and yet she testi-
> fied [more than a year later]:—
>
> The man that appeared between the back of the front seat and the
> back seat was a man slightly taller than the witness. He weighed possibly
> from 140 to 145 pounds. He was muscular, an active-looking man. His
> left hand was a good-sized hand, a hand that denoted strength.
>
> Q. The hand you said you saw where?
> A. The left hand that was placed on the back of the front seat.
> He had a gray, what I thought was a shirt, had a grayish, like navy
> color—and the face was what we would call clear-out, clean-cut face.
> Through here [indicating] was a narrow, just a little narrow. . . . The
> forehead was high. The hair brushed back and it was between, I should
> think, two inches and two and one-half inches in length and had dark
> eyebrows, but the complexion was white, peculiar white, that looked
> greenish.

The startling acuity of Miss Splaine's version was, in fact, the product of a year's recollection. . . . Let Dr. Morton Prince, professor of abnormal and dynamic psychology at Harvard University comment on this testimony:

"I do not hesitate to say that the star witness of the government testified, honestly enough, no doubt, to what was psychologically impossible. Miss Splaine testified that she had seen Sacco at the time of the shooting from the distance of about 60 feet for from 1½ to 3 seconds in a motor car going at an increasing rate of speed at about 15 to 18 miles an hour; that she saw and at the end of the year she remembered and described 16 different details of his person, even to the size of his hand, the length of his hair as being between 2 and 2½ inches long and the shade of his eyebrows! Such perception and memory under such conditions can be easily proven to be psychologically impossible."[19]

After the witnesses have finished testifying, first for the defense and then for the prosecution, each side then summarizes its case. The judge then charges the jury. In his charge to the jury he discusses the charge, the evidence introduced, the relevant features of the criminal law, and what verdicts the jury may properly return. The jury now retires to try to reach a unanimous verdict.

The Verdict

One of the more fascinating puzzles of human behavior is how 12 adult strangers forming a jury, faced with ambiguous, often conflicting testimony and evidence, are able in over 95 percent of all cases to agree unanimously upon a verdict. Because verdicts are reached in private and can be based on whim or bias, all, any, or none of the evidence presented during the trial may influence the decision of the jury. Obviously there are features of the criminal law and the administration of the law that limit the irrational decisions that the jury can render. If the presiding judge decides that the prosecution has not made a prima-facie case, he will instruct the jury to return an acquittal verdict. Additionally, his charge to the jury specifically mentions the only possible verdicts the jury can return. Some evidence exists that prestige, social-class, position, verbal facility, and the "power situations operating in the community" all affect the jury's decision.[20] Some verdicts are compromises or surrenders, where at least one juror was uncertain that the final verdict was correct but nevertheless voted with the others because of the operation of certain factors not related to the defendant's guilt or innocence. Rarely is the evidence of such a nature that when it is rationally evaluated all uncertainty disappears and the decision is without question the only one that could possibly have been made. Unfortunately, trials usually produce conflicting witnesses, circumstantial evidence, and uncertainty as to the meaning of "reasonable doubt." Perhaps the best that can be hoped for is an objective appraisal of all evidence which *reduces* some of the ambiguity, so that the verdict is the most reasonable one possible under the particular circumstances of the case.

Sentence and Appeal

If the defendant is found guilty, he is a criminal: our primary object of interest. The judge now decides, within statutory limits, what punishment he deems most appropriate. After sentence is passed, most convictions are appealed to a review (appellate) court. An appellate court will overrule a conviction not because it disagrees with the verdict but because somewhere in the procedure a "substantial error of law" has taken place, such as the defendant's not being present at all times during his trial, the jury's receiving evidence outside of court, misconduct by the jurors or by the district attorney, an error by the trial judge in some important ruling during the trial or in his charge to the jury, or some substantial error in the bill of indictment.

Conclusions

This extremely brief examination of the process of criminal procedure and the powers and responsibilities of those involved may present a picture of a system of justice which, while perhaps clumsy and duplicative, nevertheless seems an admirably fair and judicious method of establishing guilt or innocence. A frank appraisal not of the offices but of the incumbents is unlikely to produce equal complacency. The magistrate is usually elected to office;

he often has fixed political ties, and is almost never trained in the law—although subtle legal issues frequently arise in his court. As a result, the magistrate is the object of widespread public contempt. A visit to his court is likely to reveal it to be a gaudy carnival, untidy, noisy, and lacking in decorum, with an occasional scent of corruption in the air. The prosecuting attorney is also an elected official; he is, more often than not, highly ambitious, considering his current office merely as a steppingstone either to the judiciary or to higher political preferment. The judiciary, all too often, has become a comfortable sinecure for faithful and "deserving" party members at the end of their political careers. This is particularly unfortunate because it damages the generally high regard with which this branch of government is held. To these imperfections we might add condemnations of the operation of grand juries and trial juries: they are often slow, inefficient, expensive, irrational, etc.

Dilemma

The essential purpose of criminal procedure, quite simply, is to uncover the truth, to determine whether persons suspected of having committed crimes are guilty or innocent. There are, however, ethical and legal limitations to the manner in which this end may be pursued. The Anglo-Saxon tradition of law is founded on the idea of equal justice to all and operates within an adversary system of justice in which there is presumption of innocence and the burden of proof falls upon the state. If any doubt remains concerning the guilt of the defendant, he must be set free.

In actual practice these ideals are all too often not realized. Thus we are slowly coming to acknowledge one of the most obvious failures: that the poor do not in fact receive equal justice under the law. A recent report by the Attorney General demonstrates, if such a demonstration was really required, the need for adequate representation, release on bail, and access to appellate review for the impoverished.[21]

Transcending this is a larger issue, touched upon in the previous chapter, involving the problems of conflicts between the requirements of public safety and the need to protect individual liberties. The question now is not simply the rational limits of the power of the police but the requirements of our political system in adequately protecting its citizens. Every society, of necessity, must choose to operate at some point between the anarchy of completely untrammeled individual activities and a completely repressive, authoritarian "police state." Even the most dedicated libertarians agree to the need for some restrictions on human behavior, and those disposed toward wider control over the individual acknowledge the necessity of retaining many personal rights.

The balance that has evolved in America is now being seriously questioned. How can we best protect the members of society and, at the same time, retain all constitutional civil liberties? Recent Supreme Court decisions restricting police practices, narrowing the range of permissible evidence, and requiring counsel for all defendants have been sharply attacked as being overly concerned with "unbridled" civil liberties and insufficiently concerned with the general welfare. It has even been argued that our crime rates are soaring and that there is an increasing fear of "crime in the streets" as a direct and inevitable consequence of the restrictions on the police and prosecutors by a "bleeding-heart" judiciary.[22] That there has been an increase in crime is debatable, and the premise that there is a causal connection between appellate decisions and the crime rate is extremely suspect. Yet discontent and apprehension remain, and to many the restriction or redefinition of certain constitutional guarantees offers a simple and "obvious" solution to crime in the United States. The dilemma arises from the fact that we cannot simultaneously "best protect" society and maintain maximum civil liberties and procedural safeguards. Occasionally it may be impossible to prove the guilt of an offender without violating his civil rights. Providing a destitute suspect with a lawyer might result in his being set free despite his guilt. The central issue is this: How many individual rights are we willing to sacrifice to maximize the conviction of criminals? Or, conversely: How much unpunished crime will we accept to ensure the maintainance of basic civil liberties?

7

PREVENTION, IMPRISONMENT, ANNIHILATION

Crime and delinquency are probably like death and taxes, inevitable facts of life. If only for self-protection, society must react in some rational manner against the depredations of the criminal.

The perfect solution, of course, would be the prevention or significant reduction of deviant behavior, and certainly many serious attempts have been made along these lines. It would be an enormous task to synthesize and evaluate current projects. (The Office of Juvenile Delinquency and Youth Development and the President's Committee on Juvenile Delinquency alone sponsor dozens of diverse training and action programs.) Instead, one older project will be examined in detail. The Cambridge-Somerville experiment was selected for several reasons: it was longitudinal in design; it was based on a hypothesis which, a priori, seemed probably valid; and it was subjected to an admirably careful and thorough evaluation by one of its coauthors in the last stages of its operation.

An Experiment in the Prevention of Delinquency[1]

One of the most careful delinquency action programs, the Cambridge-Somerville experiment, was based on the premise that a maladjusted and therefore potentially delinquent boy needs, most of all, an adult friend (a "sustained friendly ego ideal") who might discover the causes of his problems and bring about salutary changes. The study, undertaken in 1935, began by securing from principals, schoolteachers, and several social agencies a list of all known "difficult" boys, none of whom were yet official delinquents, who lived in Cambridge and Somerville, Massachusetts. The boys had engaged in truancy, bullying, smoking, cruelty, obscenity, and the like. A vast amount of information was then collected for each of the 1,935 boys, from psychological tests, physical examinations, home-visit schedules, questionnaires, teachers' interviews and reports, and other official records. To reduce the study to no more than 650 subjects, the original population was screened by "pre-selectors" who eliminated all boys over 12 years of age as well as those who had moved or could not be located. The remaining names and records were then given to a selection committee which rated, on an 11-point scale, each boy's relative delinquency potential. Two psychologists matched equivalent pairs of boys from the subject population of 650. For each pair a coin was tossed to determine which boy would be put into the treatment group and which into the control group. Ten workers were each assigned 33 to 35 cases from the treatment group while the control group was let alone. The case load proved too heavy; in 1941, therefore, 65 boys were "retired" from the study after receiving 2½ years of treatment. The remaining 260 were further diminished by death and movement away from Cambridge-Somerville; those who were thus removed from the project had been involved for slightly over 4 years. Seventy-two more cases terminated when the subjects reached 17. Finally, there were 75 boys who remained with the project to the end (December 31, 1941). The total 325 subjects had received, on the average, almost 5 years of treatment.

The treatment essentially involved the worker's attempting to maintain a close friendship with his boys; the worker was to be a sort of perceptive, well-trained "big brother," to utilize all his intelligence, knowledge, and community resources in aiding the potential delinquent. To develop close rapport he would visit the boy's home or school; in the first year an average of 34 conferences and interviews were held with each boy. Emphasis was placed on friendly relationships and "moral suasion," which attempted to develop the moral character of the boy without a hard and fast set of rules. Some boys even received financial assistance when it was considered advisable. The treatment also included school counseling, medical care, summer camping, temporary employment, family adjustment, and occasionally foster-home placement. Medical and psychiatric help, as well as occasional tutorial services, were freely offered.

It was found, first of all, that delinquency had been considerably overpredicted. The majority of the subjects who had been predicted to become delinquent did not. Only 215 of the 650 boys had police records by the time the project ended. The comparison of treatment and control groups revealed that 114 of the treatment group and 101 of the control group had delinquency records, and this led to the conclusion that the counselors had not been notably successful in preventing boys from committing delinquencies which the police detected. Each delinquency was rated on a Seriousness Index, which defined "seriousness" as the way the term was "ordinarily understood" by law-enforcement authorities. Once more, only slight differences were found between the control and treatment groups. Comparison of commitments to correctional institutions showed that 23 boys from the treatment group and 22 boys from the control group were institutionalized.

Several boys had profited by having minor problems eliminated, and in a few cases counselors served as effective parent substitutes or altered some negative features within the family. More often, however, the treatment proved ineffectual, particularly when the offer of service was refused by the boy or his parents or when the efforts of the counselor were insufficient or incorrect. Counselors made several types of errors. For example, a boy requiring only a little help might be given none; or considerable aid might be called for and an insufficient amount given. Additionally, some of the subjects suffered from severe emotional maladjustment or extreme handicaps (e.g., feeblemindedness, epilepsy), which precluded much aid in a program of this sort.

The Cambridge-Somerville study concluded that the successfully treated case had to represent a unique combination of features: any emotional maladjustment must not have been severe; the boy (and his parents) must have desired help; and the counselor's services must have been consistent and skillfully applied. At one point in the study it is suggested that the hypothesis that a sustained friendly ego ideal is an effective preventative to delinquency might prove to be "only partially correct," benefiting most those who had already established strong positive relationships with their parents. The final appraisal holds, more pessimistically, that the basic hypothesis "appeared to be disproved."

Few, if any, prevention programs have produced what might be truly called encouraging results. Criminal behavior, as measured by court statistics of persons convicted or prison statistics of inmate populations, is certainly not on the decline. Punishment, thus, is still a very relevant issue. Criminals, voluntary violators of the important prohibitions of their society, must be punished. The pain of loss of property, liberty, or life is deliberately inflicted upon the offender, and in some way the punishment is supposed to be commensurate with the seriousness of the offense.

In courts in the United States the most usual punishment meted out is imprisonment. But certainly the judicial decision to institutionalize does not represent an ideal societal reaction to crime. If it were to be held that prison discipline imposes real suffering and at the same time educates and establishes useful and noncriminal habits that will be maintained even after release from prison, there would have to be an implicit belief that a Pavlovian scheme of conditioning, involving strict coercive regimentation of every aspect of the inmate's daily life, will necessarily produce, in time, increased respect for law and order. But life in prison, as will be seen, is far more involved than any such simple model suggests. The social interaction among prisoners and between the inmates and the custodial staff is as complex and devious as any set of relationships known to the social scientist. For example, it would be naïve and grossly erroneous to believe that the guard unilaterally exercises limitless and absolute control over a sort of inmate-slave. *The Society of Captives,* the most sophisticated analysis yet made of the prison as a community, offers a persuasive picture of the inner workings of the inmate subculture at the New Jersey State Prison at Trenton.

The Society of Captives[2]

Gresham M. Sykes' study was undertaken after he was permitted to examine the institution's files and records and to interview some guards, work supervisors, and selected inmates. The inmates at Trenton were all males, with a median age of 35; 62 percent were white; and, although 63 percent had less than 9 years of schooling, the majority had average or above-average intelligence scores. The prison is a maximum-security institution, with 24 percent of the inmates serving time for felonious homicide, 25 percent for burglary, and 20 percent for robbery.

The custodial staff are required to perform a variety of contradictory tasks. The "task of custody," i.e., the prevention of escapes, is the dominant concern of the prison officials; for they can maintain their present occupational eminence only as long as they successfully maintain their custodial function. Escape is a constant threat despite the wall and guns and guards. Continuous vigilance, involving searches, hunts, probes, and attempts to guess who are the security risks, becomes part of the normal, daily operation of the maximum-security correctional institution.

The task of maintaining internal order is difficult, because inmates are invariably granted some degree of freedom within the prison. This creates settings in which inmate crimes become possible, even likely, considering the assortment of the insane and near-insane, mental defectives, psychopaths, homosexual punks and wolves, escape artists, and agitators in the population. Repressive measures are necessary despite their tendency to increase an already existing antipathy between guards and prisoners. Elaborate regulations are imposed upon the prisoner in an attempt to restrict all acts which may endanger custody and cause internal unrest. Such extensive regimentation is attacked because of the trivial nature of so many prison regulations. Unlike the "outside" world, the prison punishes behavior which *might* lead to harmful consequences; continued order is so highly prized that the price paid in terms of inmate subjugation to minute regulations is considered acceptable.

Sykes contends that preoccupation with "self-maintenance" results in the loss of the prisoner's autonomy, which in turn impedes his chances of becoming self-sufficient, since prison labor must take place within a relaxed, permissive atmosphere if it is to be profitable. The New Jersey State Prison manufactures auto license tags, clothing, and office furniture, which can be purchased only by the state government. This employs about half of the prisoners; the other half ("Idle Men") have no regular jobs. Unfortunately, no agreement has been reached on whether prison labor is a duty, a privilege, an economic necessity, or a method of rehabilitation. The work itself is seldom done conscientiously—not surprisingly, when the wages range from 10 to 35 cents a day—and generally require no talent or skill. Praise or recognition by custodians for good work has negligible value, and indeed such recognition may provoke hostility from fellow captives. Also, what additional sanctions could be imposed on prisoners not motivated to work? Physical violence or starvation on one hand, or increased financial rewards or status symbols on the other, do not immediately offer themselves.

The task of punishment involves the paradox that persons are incarcerated as a punishment while at the same time it is felt that custodial institutions should not hurt captives beyond the pain of confinement itself. Many aspects of prison life penalize the inmates. Buildings are old and in poor condition; poor sanitation, rats, and sewer gas are continual problems. Prisoners come to believe that most administrative rules exist purely as forms of additional punishment. Sykes feels that officials are not hostile, but merely indifferent, and often are driven to using threats of further restrictions of already reduced diets and visiting privileges.

The task of reform is pursued to the extent of hiring counselors, chaplains, psychologists, and teachers; but allegiance to the goal of rehabilitation remains primarily on the verbal level: imprisonment is thought successful if the offender does not become worse. Sykes cites a warden's report which declares that what is crucial is not so much the education, recreation, or consultation the inmate receives, but how he manages to live and relate to other inmates within the institution.

The Trenton prison is bureaucratically organized, with limited and specific rules, defined areas of competence and responsibility, impersonal standards of performance, and a highly stratified series of ranks. It seems to be a world in which the rulers and their functionaries exercise extraordinary power over those who must comply with their dictates. They control, guard, watch, search, grant rewards, and inflict punishment; and the prisoner cannot escape from the system. This "almost infinite power," however, cannot be exercised independently of any rights or demands of those ruled; neither by right nor by intention are officials free from currently operating norms and laws which limit their behavior. Indeed, a variety of forces operate to undermine the power of the custodial bureaucracy. Power is based on authority when someone is recognized by others as having the *right* to exercise this power and there is on the part of the ruled a sense of *duty to comply*. The latter prerequisite is crucial and is *not* found among the prisoners. If it is suspected that the inmates could be forced to obey and that any lack of moral compulsion to obey can safely be ignored, an examination of the capability of the custodial staff to coerce prisoners physically proves this to be mistaken. The high ratio of inmates to guards, the likelihood that violence would provoke further violence, and the fact that force can be applied to only a few prisoners at any one time confirm the impossibility of complete coercion. Control by promises and threats is also ineffectual. Punishments capable of being inflicted are not profoundly different from the usual state of prison life; and extra rewards are largely nonexistent, mail, visiting, and recreational privileges all being granted to prisoners when they first arrive at the institution. Even "good time" (statutory reduction of sentence based on good behavior) automatically begins when the prisoner enters the prison. Much deviant behavior occurs within a social system where rulers seem to possess infinite control but the system of power proves defective when the captives feel no compulsion to comply and the administration is unwilling or unable to rule. The relationship between guard and prisoner is the clearest example of this situation. Although the guard may be thought of as policeman-foreman, he is often reluctant to punish all infractions of institution regulations; indeed, he may illicitly transmit information to prisoners, neglect basic security requirements, or even criticize the administrative staff. To all outward appearance a guard who engages in such actions may seem to have been corrupted by the prisoners, but this may not involve his having been bribed. The guard is occupationally required to be in close, intimate association with convicts, and he can remain aloof only with the greatest difficulty; he cannot withdraw, and there are no intermediaries between him and the inmates. American society places a premium on being a "nice guy," and the guard, not immune to this cultural demand, can be morally blackmailed by the prisoners, who will ridicule him for not being a nice guy. Because he is intermediate in the bureaucracy, midway between the prisoners and the higher-level administrators, the guard frequently demonstrates mixed loyalties, particularly when unhappy with the policy makers; and the inmates listen willingly and sympathetically. It is also important that although the prisoners have been called evil and are being punished by society, they may have been more financially successful than the guard; therefore, the guard may secretly admire and respect his notorious captives.

The guard cannot strictly enforce all rules if he expects any reciprocity from the inmates. He is dependent on them for the successful performance of his duties: a troublesome cellblock reflects negatively on the guard's ability to perform his job. He also wants to win compliance where it counts and get into the prisoners' good graces; for he may be a hostage one day, and how he has treated his prisoners might have a bearing on what would happen to him then. Additionally, inmates may innocently encroach upon custodial duties. They freely engage in a variety of minor chores and increasingly take over many of the guard's minor tasks. The indifferent, lazy, or naïve guard may find that much of his power has somehow slipped from his grasp. When assigned to a new cellblock the custodian is faced with previous relationships which operated between the previous guard and the inmates, and it requires a good deal of moral courage to defy this precedent.

The lack of any moral obligation to obey prison rules, obvious limits to coercive power, emphasis on punishment and not on rewards, and the elements tending to corrupt the guard (friendship, reciprocity, and transference of duties to trusted inmates) are all latent defects that are not due to personal insufficiencies but rather operate within the institutional system of power.

The prison is an unpleasant place at best; the inmate's life is one of continual pain. There is, first of all, the deprivation of liberty. The prisoner's life is restricted to an area of a little over 13 acres, within which movement is strictly controlled; loss of freedom involves confinement *to* an institution and confinement *within* an institution. The prisoner is cut off from family and friends, and this "involuntary seclusion" results in lost emotional ties and a lonely and boring existence.

The prisoner is also deprived of goods and services. No inmate owns any furniture or clothing. What is given to him is given temporarily and is meant to identify him as a criminal. True, his basic physiological needs are met, but the ways in which they are met merely contribute to his drab life. The painful thing is that he can not secure such things as cigarettes, liquor, interesting food, and different clothing, which give life some flavor. Inmates often regard their poverty not as punishment for their criminal behavior but as a manifestation of the state's hypocritical tyranny.

Loss of heterosexual relationships is another serious deprivation. The authorities act as though inmates somehow adapt to prison life with lessened sex drive and therefore suffer from relatively little frustration. Actually, this is nonsense, of course; frustration, physiological and psychological, is deep and constantly present.

The prisoner's loss of autonomy involves his being forced to abide by a series of rules and demands which control the most intimate aspects of his life. He eats, sleeps, works, and spends his leisure according to administrative dictates. Most prison regulations are considered by the prisoners to be meaningless gestures of authoritarian control. Few prison officials will justify any regulation; this would imply that inmates have a right to know why an act is prohibited, and that in turn would mean that if the explanations were inadequate the rule would or should be changed. The curtailing of the inmate's decision-making role and the lack of any explanation for commands threaten to destroy the prisoner's self-image and to revert him to the dependent status of childhood.

Finally, the deprivation of security forces the offender to associate involuntarily with other serious criminals for long periods of time. As one prisoner said, "The worst thing about prison is you have to live with other prisoners." Living in an inmate world, each convict is aware that he will one day be "tested," pushed by others to see how far they can go before he will fight. If he doesn't fight, he becomes an object of contempt; if he fights and wins, he becomes an inviting target for all prisoners who want to enhance their prestige—a situation which perhaps parallels the western legend of the old, tired gunfighter reluctantly forced to kill ambitious young gunmen eager to make a "reputation."

Sykes believes that the main purpose of inmate cant or argot is not to maintain secrecy of communication nor to serve as a distinguishing symbol of group loyalty and membership; it is a separate language which orders and codifies experience within an institutional framework. People assign special distinctive names to important social roles, and these names act as shorthand indicators of those roles and the statuses attached to them. These labels analyze and classify behavior and individuals and carry the penumbra of admiration or disapproval.

In the inmate subculture there are "rats" or "squealers," men who betray fellow captives by giving information to the custodial staff. These terms are never used jokingly, for they represent the most serious accusation and are descriptive of the most reprehensible behavior that can be attributed to a fellow inmate; such a person has betrayed the entire prisoner population. "Rats" are of two types: those who reveal themselves to the authorities to collect some reward (preferential treatment), and those who remain anonymous and inform for revenge or to get rid of a competitor. The "center man" gives information to the custodial staff but does not inform on others. He has acquired some of the custodial values, and he may even identify himself with the rulers; but at least his disloyalty is open, unlike the treachery of the "rat."

Occasionally prisoners monopolize scarce commodities to reduce their own private material deprivation. The "gorilla" will take by force what he wants from others. Unlike the guard, therefore, the gorilla finds violence a very potent weapon. After his reputation has been established, he can coercively exploit others by simple threats. "Merchants" exploit along different lines, by means of fraud, chicanery, or cheating. They are despised for selfishly pursuing their own interests and thriving on the misery of their companions. To them, as to the gorilla, fellow captives are objects to exploit rather than human beings.

A third set of argot roles relate to sexual behavior. A homosexual who plays the aggressively masculine role is called a "wolf"; one who is submissively feminine is a "punk" or "fag." The punk is a prisoner driven to homosexuality by temporary deprivation of heterosexual outlet, whereas the fag is a true pervert who genuinely enjoys homosexuality, affecting an effeminate walk, lip rouge, and the like. The punk simply cannot fend off the older wolves; but both he and the fag are clearly failures as men.

There are also prisoners who engage in sudden outbursts of violence, continually defy authority, and accept punishment as a natural consequence of their actions. These "ball-busters" always give guards a hard time. Disobediance and physical and verbal abuse are their normal mode of behavior. They represent a quixotic blend of courageous opposition and childish troublemaking. The ideal prisoner is cool, stoical, brave, dignified—all in all, a "real man." The "tough" is quick to quarrel with fellow prisoners. He fights constantly because of imagined insults and is regarded with fear and treated with respect. He is not really a bully, just touchy, violent, and extremely pugnacious—a "real man" turned sour. He has some real courage, unlike the "hipster," who pretends to be tough, brags, and threatens harm, but who is almost never violent.

These argot roles, excepting only the "real man," are models of behavior by which some prisoners attempt to reduce the hardships of prison life at the expense of others. They jeopardize prisoner solidarity and cohesiveness, so that as they are reduced in number prison life becomes more agreeable for the inmates.

Capital Crimes

Society not only prohibits selected forms of behavior by defining them as criminal and punishable, but it indicates their comparative seriousness by the penalties prescribed for each. Fines are levied for relatively minor offenses; imprisonment is appropriate for more serious crimes. Throughout history the most severe of punishments, the death penalty, has been prescribed for those acts considered most reprehensible and abhorrent. The Mosaic Code lists no fewer than 33 capital crimes, including witchcraft, "eating any manner of blood," using holy ointment on a stranger, and failure to keep the Passover.[3] During certain periods of the Roman republic, capital offenses included violation of vows of chastity by vestal virgins, publication of libel, and singing insulting songs. In mediaeval England, consorting with gypsies, clipping coins, and offenses against the laws of the forest all carried the penalty of death.

From the fifteenth century to the eighteenth century in England there were only 17 capital crimes. Then, in 1722, the infamous Waltham "Black" Act was passed by Parliament. According to one authority, this single piece of legislation created perhaps 350 new capital crimes, including such behavior as appearing armed or disguised on roads, open heaths, parks, and forests; stealing rabbits or fish; destroying fish ponds or trees; maiming or wounding cattle; and burning a barn or a stack of wood, corn, hay, or straw. Sections of the act remained in existence for over 110 years.[4] In Colonial America the situation was not notably different. Capital offenses included, in Massachusetts Bay Colony, idolatry, witchcraft, and a child's cursing or hitting his parents; in New Haven Colony, profaning the Lord's Day by work or sport and doing it "proudly, presumptuously and with a high head." In Virginia, any Englishman found north of the York River and any Indian found south of the James River were guilty of capital offenses.

At the present time, nine states have no capital crimes: Wisconsin (which abandoned the death penalty in 1853), Maine (1887), Minnesota (1911), Alaska (1957), Hawaii (1957), Michigan (1963), Oregon (1964), Iowa (1965), and West Virginia (1965). Two other states have capital crimes for which no one has been executed for over 30 years: Rhode Island (which prescribes capital punishment for a "lifer" who murders someone while in prison) and North Dakota (where treason and murder by a lifer are capital offenses). Of 54 American jurisdictions (the 50 states, the District of Columbia, Puerto Rico, and the Federal government in its civil and military capacities), 45 permit execution for an offender convicted of murder in one form or another; 36 for kidnapping; 22 for treason; 19 for rape; 15 for "carnal knowledge" (an omnibus offense usually involving statutory rape); 13 for robbery; and 8 for crimes of "extreme danger" (bombing, machine-gunning, etc). There are additionally a variety of crimes carrying the death penalty in individual jurisdictions; for example, forcing a woman to marry against her will (Arkansas), desecration of graves (Georgia), castration (Georgia), and "pirating" of an airplane (Federal government). With few exceptions, the sentence of death is an optional punishment; that is, the simple conviction of a capital crime does not mean that a death sentence is automatically imposed: this secondary decision must be made by the judge or jury.[5]

Relatively complete data on executions in the United States have been available only since 1930.[6] From that year to 1963, 3,833 executions took place, averaging 118 per year. For the decade of the 1930s the average per year was 167; for 1940 to 1949 it was 128; for 1950 to 1959, 72; and for 1960 through 1963 the average was only 41. Over 86 percent of all executions were for the crime of murder; 11 percent were for rape. The remaining 69 executions involved armed robbery, kidnapping, burglary, espionage, and aggravated assault by a lifer. As might be expected, considerable regional and state variations exist in the use of the death penalty. Sixty percent

(2,292) of all the executions occurred in the South (South Atlantic, East South Central, and West South Central States); and only 608 were carried out in the New England and Middle Atlantic States, although these Northeastern states, as of 1960, had only 15 percent less population than the Southern states. The five leading states— Georgia (364 executions), New York (329), Texas (292), California (291), and North Carolina (263)—account for over 40 percent of all executions in the United States since 1930.

Fifty-four percent of all offenders put to death were Negroes. Twenty-seven percent of those executed in the Northeastern states were Negroes; 72 percent of those executed in the South were Negroes. About half of all those put to death for murder were Negroes; and Negroes accounted for no less than 90 percent of those executed for rape. (The only states applying the death penalty for rape are Southern states, except for the border state of Missouri.)

Capital Punishment

Public executions have, historically, been marked by the unbridled ferocity and deliberate cruelty with which the felon was put to death. It was required that he die slowly and in great agony. The methods of execution varied, but they would all be characterized, by present-day humanitarian standards, as excessively brutal. The Bible mentions such punishments as being put to the sword, stoned, decapitated, rendered asunder, crucified, strangled, and burned to death. (Burning was used as late as 1789 in England.) Drowning was also an ancient form of punishment. The Romans executed parricides by putting the murderer into a bag with a dog, a cock, a viper, and an ape, and throwing the menagerie into the Tiber.

In mediaeval Europe male felons were often broken on the wheel. In the final form of this punishment, the executioner, using a metal bar, would break the criminal's arms, legs, thighs, and ribs or pelvis, then drape the broken body around the rim of a wagon wheel where it remained until death brought relief. At this same time caste differences arose regarding the method of execution. Condemned members of the nobility were permitted the relatively quick death of decapitation (the quickness was largely dependent, of

course, on the strength, coordination, and experience of the heads-
man); whereas commoners were hanged—a slow, ghastly form of
strangulation. Minor alterations in the technique of hanging made
it somewhat less horrible; but it was not until the nineteenth century,
with the development of the "drop," that hanging brought quick
death. It had been calculated that if a criminal with a noose properly
placed around his neck were suddenly to drop a certain distance (the
precise length of the fall being determined by the height, weight,
and physical condition of the condemned man), a cervical vertebrae
would be crushed, the spinal cord severed, and death would result
almost instantaneously. Beheadings similarly underwent considerable technological improvement with the invention, in the eighteenth
century, of the first really efficient beheading machine. Dr. Guillotin
humanely proposed that hanging and decapitation by means of the
axe should be replaced by his swifter and more certain device. He
also suggested that all capital felons, regardless of rank or position,
be executed in the same manner.[7] America's developments in this
sanguine enterprise consist of the introduction of electrocution in
1890 and lethal gas in 1924.

History records several instances when a society, aghast at the
enormity of a particular crime—e.g., regicide—bypasses the usual
means of execution and proceeds to kill the offender with the most
savage cruelty it is capable of inflicting. Probably the most stupefy-
ing execution in modern times was that of Francis Ravilliack for
the murder of Henry IV of France. He was drawn to his place of
execution in a tumbrel (dung cart) "to convert all bloody-minded
traytors from the like enterprise," and laid out on a St. Andrew's
cross; and then his hand (which slew the king) was put into a brimstone fire until hand and arm were consumed. Next, red-hot pincers
were used to pinch and burn his breasts, arms, thighs, legs, and other
parts of the body; after this, a mixture of scalding oil, rosin, pitch,
and brimstone was poured into his open wounds. A rundle of clay
with a hole in its middle was placed upon his navel, and into this
molten lead was poured. Finally, four strong horses were tied to his
four limbs, so as to tear his body into quarters. But his flesh and

joints were "strongly . . . knit together," and the horses could not pull the joints out. A sympathetic bystander was moved to cut the flesh under his arms and thighs so that his body would be more easily torn to pieces. This proved successful, and thereupon he was pulled apart and died; but the viewing mob, enraged by this abrupt ending to their amusement, snatched the dismembered corpse from the executioner and beat some parts of the body to pieces on the ground and slashed other parts into thin slivers, so that nothing was left but the bare bones. These were collected and burned to cinders, and the ashes were scattered into the wind, "as being thought to be unworthy of the earthly burial."[8] In the twentieth century, the general reaction to such barbarity is one of extreme revulsion, for today executions are quietly and swiftly performed within the confines of a prison in as painless a manner as possible. Still, in modern times we must remember recent systematic efforts to annihilate millions of people considered undesirable, and governments which to this day condone physical torture when it is thought to be in the best interests of the state.

Retention or Abolition   Endlessly argued, passionately debated, and seldom resolved to anyone's complete satisfaction, capital punishment remains one of our minor cultural preoccupations. Professor Thorsten Sellin divides the various· points of view into dogmas and utilitarian (scientific) arguments. Dogmas are rationales which are accepted (or rejected) on the basis of faith, for they are incapable of being *proved* true or false. Thus, some hold that the death penalty is the only *just* penalty, or that it is more *humane* than life imprisonment, or that man does not have the right to take anyone's life. The concept of *evidence* does not seem to apply to such matters as justice, morality, or the inherent rights of man; on the other hand, it does apply in the case of the utilitarian beliefs.

Arguments for Retention   One occasionally hears that after a particularly atrocious crime an aroused public would take matters into its own hands and lynch the criminal if the death penalty was not available. Evidence clearly shows, however, that lynchings, by and large, have taken place in those states which have numerous capital crimes and which have demonstrated no reluctance to execute.

The old nonsense that the death penalty prevents the continuation of a bad hereditary strain is still circulating. To this it may be replied that the genetic basis of criminal behavior is completely unsupported at the present time. Moreover, even if it were proven, would not sterilization prove equally effective in halting the transmission of hereditary flaws?

Should we not be concerned with the fact that it is more economical to execute than to keep a serious offender in prison for years? Should the public be unnecessarily burdened by higher taxes in order to maintain a dangerous criminal when it can be spared that cost by his death? Prisoners are not self-sufficient, because prison labor is specifically designed not to show a profit—a policy that satisfies both labor and management. It may be argued that execution is not justified because political decisions have resulted in a deliberately expensive system of imprisonment. Further, it could be argued that if financial cost is a major criterion for the existence of the death penalty, an enormously greater saving could be effected by executing institutionalized mental defectives, who are far greater in number and who by the very nature of their illness are likely to remain financial burdens their entire lives.

Perhaps the death penalty is the only *real* protection for society; for if the murderer is sent to prison, even for life, he will in all liklihood be released one day and return to his life of crime. Existing data reveal, however, that only a small percentage of all persons who have been convicted of capital crimes and who *could* have received the death penalty were sentenced to death, and of those sentenced only a minority were actually executed. Additionally, numerous studies have shown that the murderer and rapist are among the *least* recividistic of all criminals. If what is desired is protection against the serious "repeater," burglars are a much more likely target, being more likely to recidivate and representing a larger proportion of the total criminal population than murderers and rapists combined.

Arguments for Abolition The Marquis de Lafayette once said, "I shall ask for the abolition of the penalty of death until I have the infallibility of human judgment demonstrated to me." Irreparable errors of justice associated with capital punishment remain a telling argument to this day. If a prisoner is found to be innocent, a contrite society may release the unfortunate man and assuage its conscience by offering some compensation to him; but what remedy can there be if innocence is established after the offender has been put to death? Far too many cases exist in which it appears that individuals were executed who were certainly innocent or whose guilt does not seem to have been established beyond a reasonable doubt.[9] A close examination of statistics seems to confirm another argument of abolitionists: that the death penalty operates primarily against the poor, the lower classes, and the socially despised ethnic and racial groups.

Deterrence Deterrence is the major argument of both those who would abolish the death penalty and those who would retain it. On the one hand, it is said that the death penalty uniquely deters the potential murderer and rapist; on the other hand, it is argued that life imprisonment works just as well.

Some studies have analyzed the number of murders in an area prior and subsequent to highly publicized executions or sentencings to death. Robert Dann examined the homicide rate in Philadelphia 60 days before and 60 days after a heavily publicized simultaneous execution of four local murderers and found no significant differences between the two periods. He concluded that the actual example of the execution of several felons did not appreciably deter others from committing murder.[10] A later investigation of Philadelphia data, using somewhat more precise definitions than Dann's, also found no differences in murder rates 8 weeks before and after four widely reported sentencings to death from 1944 to 1947.[11] William Graves produced similar findings regarding homicide rates 3 days before and 3 days after selected executions in several counties in California from 1946 to 1955.[12]

Another method of analysis is based on the assumption that the murder rate should be lower in states having the death penalty than in bordering states that are similar in population characteristics and general socioeconomic conditions but do not have capital punishment. A comparison was made of the homicide rates of Maine (no death penalty) with New Hampshire and Vermont; Massachusetts and Connecticut with Rhode Island (death penalty only for certain inmates who commit murder); Michigan (death penalty only for treason at the time of the study) with Ohio and Indiana; Minnesota (no death penalty) with Wisconsin and Iowa; and finally North Dakota with South Dakota and Nebraska. It was determined that in no instance did a state without the death penalty have a higher rate than a neighboring state with the death penalty.[13]

One final piece of research examined changes in the homicide rates of states which had the death penalty, abolished it, and later reintroduced it.[14]

1. Arizona's homicide rate from December, 1916, to December, 1918, when murder was not punishable by death, was 46. During the 2 years immediately prior to abolition, it was 41; and for the 2 years after the death penalty was reintroduced (December, 1918), it was 45.

2. The murder rate in Colorado was 16.3 for the years 1891 to 1896. During the period of abolition (1897 to 1900), the figure rose slightly to 18; but for the first 5 years after the death penalty was reintroduced (1901 to 1905) it was 19.

3. For 1866 to 1871, the murder rate in Iowa was only 2.6. During the following years of abolition (1872 to 1878), the figure rose to 8.8; but from 1878 to 1885, with capital punishment reinstated, it continued to rise to 13.1.

4. Missouri's murder rate from 1912 to 1916 was between 7.8 and 10. From the time the death penalty was abolished in April, 1917, to July, 1919, the rate was slightly under 11; and when capital punishment was reinstated from 1919 to 1924, the average came to 11.5.

5. Oregon had 59 murders between 1910 and 1914, when the crime could have borne the penalty of death for the offender; whereas

during the period of abolition (1915 to 1920) only 36 murders took place.

6. The state of Washington's homicide rate for the years of capital punishment, 1902 to 1911, was considerably lower than for the years of abolition between 1913 and March, 1919. After the death penalty had been brought back, the proportion of murders continued to rise.

7. The average murder rate in Kansas from 1930 to 1935 (when Kansas had no capital crimes) was considerably higher than during the first 5 years after the death penalty was reintroduced (1935 to 1940).

8. South Dakota's murder rate was the same during the period of no capital punishment (1934 to 1939) as in the first 5 years after capital punishment was reintroduced (1939 to 1944).

Thus in seven out of eight cases (the exception being the experience of Kansas), the homicide rates during periods of abolition were equalled or exceeded when capital punishment was reintroduced.

Professor Thorsten Sellin's statement to the British Royal Commission on Capital Punishment still remains probably the most accurate evaluation of the deterrent effect of capital punishment. Sellin stated that an appraisal of the available data does not permit the conclusion that the death penalty deters any better than a sentence of life imprisonment.[15]

Dilemma

Because punishment, by definition, involves the calculated infliction of pain, even to the extent of occasional executions, thought must be given to the theoretical premises which underlie our system of correction. The question may properly be raised why anyone is punished under the law. What purpose does punishment serve or should it serve: social revenge, group solidarity, or incapacitation? Is reformation a viable alternative to these? Present practices, ranging from capital punishment to probation, reflect quite different, indeed mutually contradictory objectives. What would be the consequences if only one rationale were selected and consistently applied? It will be seen that none of the objectives implies a perfect solution to the problem of punishment.

If punishment is thought to be primarily a means of social revenge and group solidarity (and as matters now stand, a powerful case could be made for this view), the deviant is made to suffer because somehow this balances the scales of justice. An offender must pay for his offense; and if the payment is appropriate (if the punishment "fits" the crime), society is appeased—it has somehow gotten even. Imposing severe penalties on criminals may also serve as a convenient and acceptable outlet for the pent-up hostilities and hatreds of the general population. Although the purgative effects may be temporary, pleasure is still derived from the knowledge that the criminal has gotten what he deserved. If the premise of retaliation were carried to its logical extreme, a code of justice founded on it would extend corporal and capital punishment, increase periods of imprisonment, and make prison life even less bearable than it presently is.

The consequences of adopting a policy of incapacitation are similar in many ways to those mentioned above, but the focus of attention would be on institutional regimentation and control. For if it is assumed that the offender is incapable of harming society only as long as he is segregated from it, maximum prison security and maximum prison sentences become the criteria of the successful correctional program. Violence would be acceptable if it resulted in a docile society of captives, but unacceptable if it produced inmates who were discontented, hostile, and prone to escape.

It might finally be argued that the concept of punishment should be abandoned and replaced by efforts to rehabilitate and treat. Within any penal system, no matter how repressive or vindictive, it must be assumed that virtually all prisoners will in time be released. Simply as a matter of rational self-interest then, we should institute programs that are most likely to reduce recidivism and best protect society. Accordingly, gratuitous brutality would be abandoned and all current procedures would be closely examined. Probably a large proportion of all prisoners would be transferred to other settings more conducive to their rehabilitation. A partial or complete abandonment of imprisonment might ensue, based, in part, on the fact that it is absurd to attempt to adjust inmates to a conventional noncriminal way of life while they are still within a community which is dominated by criminal values. One of the most interesting problems relating to the ideal of reform is whether all offenders should be equally treated regardless of the probability of success. Should it not be recognized that—given a very restricted information set, scarce resources, etc.—there will remain a residual group of offenders, "hopelessly criminal" and impervious to any foreseeable form of intervention? This recognition may lead inevitably to an American version of preventative detention in which reformation remains the general goal while incapacitation becomes the immediate objective for the intractable offenders.

FOOTNOTES

Chapter Two: Crime and Delinquency

1. William L. Clark and William L. Marshall, *A Treatise on the Law of Crimes,* 5th ed., Callaghan & Company, Chicago, 1952, pp. 1–16.
2. From a rather considerable literature on this curious and most interesting phenomenon some of the most important items are: Herbert Wechsler and Jerome Michael, "A Rationale of the Law of Homicide," *Columbia Law Review,* vol. 37, pp. 701–761, 1261–1325, May and December, 1937; Roy Moreland, *The Law of Homicide,* The Bobbs-Merrill Company, Inc., Indianapolis, 1952, chap. 6, pp. 42–54; Norval Morris, "The Felon's Responsibility for the Lethal Acts of Others," *University of Pennsylvania Law Review,* vol. 105, pp. 50–81, November, 1956.
3. John H. Wigmore, *A Kaleidoscope of Justice,* Washington Law Book Co., Washington, D.C., 1941.
4. U.S. Department of Health, Education and Welfare, Children's Bureau, *Juvenile Court Statistics, 1963,* Statistical Series, 79, 1964.
5. Thorsten Sellin, *Culture Conflict and Crime,* Social Science Research Council Bulletin 41, Social Science Research Council, New York, 1938.
6. Paul W. Tappan, "Who is the Criminal?" *American Sociological Review,* vol. 12, pp. 96–102, February, 1947.
7. Starke R. Hathaway and Elio D. Monachesi, *Adolescent Personality and Behavior: MMPI Patterns of Normal, Delinquent, Dropout and Other Outcomes,* The University of Minnesota Press, Minneapolis, 1963, pp. 76–78.
8. F. Ivan Nye, *Family Relationships and Delinquent Behavior,* John Wiley & Sons, Inc., New York, 1958, pp. 10–19.

Chapter Three: Sources of Information

1. U.S. Federal Bureau of Investigation, *Crime in the United States: Uniform Crime Reports, 1963,* 1964, table 22, p. 108.
2. *Ibid.,* table 25, p. 111.
3. *Ibid.,* p. 45.
4. U.S. Department of Justice, Federal Bureau of Prisons, *Characteristics of State Prisoners, 1960,* National Prisoner Statistics, n.d.
5. U.S. Federal Bureau of Investigation, *op. cit.,* table 11, p. 97.
6. Thorsten Sellin, "The Significance of Records of Crime," *The Law Quarterly Review,* vol. 67, pp. 489–504, 1951.

7. Courtlandt C. Van Vechten, "Differential Criminal Case Mortality in Selected Jurisdictions," *American Sociological Review*, vol. 7, pp. 833–839, December, 1942.

8. Federal Bureau of Investigation, *op. cit.*, table 11, p. 97.

9. Bernard Lander, *Towards an Understanding of Juvenile Delinquency*, Columbia University Press, New York, 1954.

10. William M. Bates, "The Ecology of Juvenile Delinquency in St. Louis," unpublished doctoral dissertation, George Washington University, St. Louis, Mo., 1959.

11. William M. Bates and Thomas McJunkins, "Vandalism and Status Differences," *The Pacific Sociological Review*, vol. 5, pp. 89–92, Fall, 1962.

12. David J. Bordua, "Juvenile Delinquency and 'Anomie'. An Attempt at Replication," *Social Problems*, vol. 6, pp. 230–238, Winter, 1958–1959.

13. Kenneth Polk, "Juvenile Delinquency and Social Areas," *Social Problems*, vol. 5, pp. 214–217, Winter, 1957–1958.

14. J. J. Conlin, "An Area Study of Juvenile Delinquency in Baltimore, Maryland: A Retest of Lander's Theses and a Test of Cohen's Hypotheses," unpublished doctoral dissertation, St. Louis University, St. Louis, Mo., 1961.

15. R. J. Chilton, "Continuities in Delinquency Area Research: A Comparison of Studies for Baltimore, Detroit and Indianapolis," *American Sociological Review*, pp. 71–83, February, 1964.

16. Leonard Savitz, *Delinquency and Migration*, Commission on Human Relations, Philadelphia, 1960.

Chapter Four: Sociological Theories of Delinquency

1. Richard Dugdale, *The Jukes: A Study in Crime, Pauperism, and Heredity*, G. P. Putnam's Sons, New York, 1877; Arthur H. Estabrook, *The Jukes in 1915*, Carnegie Institution, Washington, D.C., 1916; Henry H. Goddard, *The Kallikaks*, The Macmillan Company, New York, 1912.

2. The central work, without question, is Cesare Lombroso, *L'Uomo Delinquente*, 2d ed., Bocca, Turin, 1878. In English there is Gina Lombroso Ferrero, *Criminal Man According to the Classification of Cesare Lombroso*, G. P. Putnam's Sons, New York, 1911. The theory was heavily attacked by Charles Goring, *The English Convict*, His Majesty's Stationery Office, London, 1913, and was unsuccessfully resurrected by Ernest A. Hooton, in his *Crime and the Man*, Harvard University Press, Cambridge, Mass., 1939.

3. Goring, *Ibid*.
4. Among others, the most important are Johannes Lange, *Crime and Destiny*, Boni, New York, 1930; and A. J. Rosanoff, L. M. Handy and I. A. Rosanoff, "Etiology of Child Behavior Difficulties, Juvenile Delinquency and Adult Criminality," *Psychiatric Monographs*, no. 1, California Department of Institutions, Sacramento, Calif., 1941.
5. William Healy and Augusta F. Bronner, *New Light on Delinquency and Its Treatment*, Yale University Press, New Haven, Conn., 1936, is probably the most cited study along these lines.
6. Karl F. Schuessler and Donald R. Cressey, "Personality Characteristics of Criminals," *American Journal of Sociology*, vol. 55 pp. 476–484, July–August, 1953.
7. Starke R. Hathaway and Elio D. Monachesi, *Adolescent Personality and Behavior: MMPI Patterns of Normal, Delinquent, Dropout and Other Outcomes*, The University of Minnesota Press, Minneapolis, 1963, tables 107–110, pp. 170–171.
8. Robert K. Merton, "Social Structure and Anomie," *American Sociological Review*, vol. 3, pp. 672–682, October, 1938; extended in Robert K. Merton, *Social Theory and Social Structure*, The Free Press of Glencoe, New York, 1949, pp. 125–149; and further elaborated in the 1957 edition of *Social Theory and Social Structure*.
9. Solomon Kobrin, "The Conflict of Values in Delinquency Areas," *American Sociological Review*, vol. 16, pp. 653–661, October, 1951.
10. Note the similar results in the study *Migration and Delinquency*, discussed in chap. 4.
11. Albert K. Cohen, *Delinquent Boys*, The Free Press of Glencoe, New York, 1955.
12. Gresham A. Sykes and David Matza, "Techniques of Neutralization: A Theory of Delinquency," *American Sociological Review*, vol. 22, pp. 664–670, December, 1957.
13. Albert K. Cohen and James F. Short, Jr., "Research in Delinquent Subcultures," *The Journal of Social Issues*, vol. 14, no. 3, pp. 20–37, 1958.
14. Richard A. Cloward and Lloyd E. Ohlin, *Delinquency and Opportunity*, The Free Press of Glencoe, New York, 1961.
15. Clifford R. Shaw and Henry D. McKay. *Juvenile Delinquency and Urban Areas*, The University of Chicago Press, Chicago, 1942.
16. Walter B. Miller, "Lower Class Culture as Generating Milieu of Gang Delinquency," *The Journal of Social Issues*, vol. 14, no. 3, pp. 5–19, 1958.
17. For a rather full discussion of the problem of Negro criminality see

Leonard D. Savitz, *Crime and the American Negro,* The Free Press of Glencoe, New York, forthcoming.

Chapter Five: Law Enforcement in America

1. Few agencies of the Federal government have been subjected to such violent attack or defended with such passion as the Bureau of Investigation. Putting the agency on the side of the angels is Don Whitehead, *The FBI Story,* Random House, Inc., New York, 1956; viewing them in a more diabolic light is Fred J. Cook, *The FBI Nobody Knows,* The Macmillan Company, New York, 1964.
2. Albert J. Reiss, *Occupation and Social Status,* The Free Press of Glencoe, New York, 1961.
3. August Vollmer et al., *Report on Police,* National Commission on Law Observance and Enforcement, Report 14, 1931.
4. Fred Imbau and John E. Reid, *Lie Detection and Criminal Interrogation,* The Williams & Wilkins Company, Baltimore, 1953.
5. Special Committee to Investigate Organized Crime in Interstate Commerce, *Third Interim Report,* United States Senate No. 307, 82d Cong., 1951, pp. 184–185.
6. The infrequent policeman who engages in crime has been dealt with, in a highly popular manner, in W. T. Brannon, *The Crooked Cops,* Regency Books, Evanston, Ill., 1962, and Ralph Lee Smith, *The Tarnished Badge,* Thomas Y. Crowell Company, New York, 1965.
7. The Institute of Public Administration, *Crime Records in Police Management,* New York, 1952. Sections reprinted in Marvin E. Wolfgang, Leonard Savitz, and Norman Johnston, *The Sociology of Crime and Delinquency,* John Wiley & Sons, Inc., New York, 1962, pp. 56–58.
8. Wayne R. LaFave, "The Police and Nonenforcement of the Law— Part I," *Wisconsin Law Review,* vol. 1962, no. 1, pp. 104–137, January, 1962; and "The Police and Nonenforcement of the Law— Part II," *Wisconsin Law Review,* vol. 1962, no. 2, pp. 179–237, March, 1962. See also Joseph J. Goldstein, "Police Discretion Not to Invoke the Criminal Process: Low-visibility Decision in the Administration of Justice," *The Yale Law Journal,* vol. 69, pp. 543–594, 1960.
9. Paula R. Markowitz and Walter I. Summerfield, Jr., "Philadelphia Police Practices and the Law of Arrest," *The University of Pennsylvania Law Review,* vol. 100, pp. 1182–1216, June, 1952.
10. *Ibid.,* p. 1206.
11. William A. Westley, "Violence and the Police," *The American Journal of Sociology,* vol. 49, pp. 34–41, August, 1953.

12. U.S. Federal Bureau of Investigation, *Crime in the United States: Uniform Crime Reports, 1963,* n.d., pp. 132–133.

13. *Mapp v. Ohio,* 81 Sup. Ct. 1684 (1961); *Escobedo v. Illinois,* 378 U.S. 478 (1964); *McNabb v. United States,* 318 U.S. 332 (1943); and *Mallory v. United States,* 354 U.S. 449 (1957).

14. A fine set of readings, easily available and impartially presenting all sides of the police controversy, are to be found in *Should Law Enforcement Agencies in the United States Be Given Greater Freedom in the Investigation and Prosecution of Crime?* Selected Excerpts and References Relating to the National Debate Proposition for American Colleges and Universities, 1965–1966. Compiled by the American Law Division of the Legislative Reference Service, Library of Congress. H. Doc. 304, 89th Cong., 1st Sess., September, 1965.

Chapter Six: From Crime to Criminal

1. Two excellent statements on the administration of justice in America are Lester O. Orfield, *Criminal Procedure from Arrest to Appeal,* New York University Press, New York, 1947, and Ernst W. Puttkammer, *The Administration of Criminal Law,* The University of Chicago Press, Chicago, 1953.

2. American Civil Liberties Union, *Secret Detention of the Chicago Police,* The Free Press of Glencoe, New York, 1959. Selections are reprinted in Norman Johnston, Leonard Savitz, and Marvin E. Wolfgang. *The Sociology of Punishment and Correction,* John Wiley & Sons, Inc., New York, 1962, pp. 12–17.

3. Puttkammer, *op. cit.,* p. 88.

4. The best recent analysis of bail practices in the United States is Daniel J. Freed and Patricia M. Wald, *Bail in the United States, 1964: A Report on the National Conference on Bail and Criminal Justice, Cosponsored by the United States Department of Justice and the Vera Foundation,* Washington, D.C., May 27–29, 1964.

5. Orfield, *op. cit.,* p. 104.

6. Caleb Foote, "The Bail System and Equal Justice," *Federal Probation,* vol. 19, pp. 43–48, September, 1955.

7. Patricia Wald, "Pretrial Detention and Ultimate Freedom: A Statistical Study—Forward," and Anne Rankin, "The Effect of Pretrial Detention," *New York University Law Review,* vol. 39, pp. 631–655, June, 1964.

8. Charles E. Ares, Anne Rankin, and Herbert Sturz, "The Manhattan Bail Project: An Interim Report on the Use of Pre-trial Parole," *New York University Law Review,* vol. 38, pp. 67–95, January, 1963.

9. *Ibid.*, table 7, p. 82, and p. 86.

10. Cited in Freed and Wald, *op. cit.*, p. 39.

11. Puttkammer, op. cit., p. 192.

12. Donald J. Newman, "Pleading Guilty for Considerations: A Study in Bargain Justice," *Journal of Criminal Law, Criminology and Police Science,* vol. 46, pp. 780–790, March–April, 1956.

13. This decision, *Gideon v. Wainright,* 372 U.S. 335 (1963), and its rather revolutionary implications is splendidly dealt with in Anthony Lewis, *Gideon's Trumpet,* Random House, Inc., New York, 1964.

14. Guy B. Johnson, "The Negro and Crime," *The Annals of the American Academy of Political and Social Science,* vol. 217, pp. 93–104, September, 1941.

15. Harold Garfinkel, "Research Note on Inter- and Intraracial Homicide," *Social Forces,* vol. 27, pp. 369–381, May, 1949.

16. J. D. Turner, "Differential Punishment in a Biracial Community," unpublished master's thesis, Indiana University, Bloomington, 1948; and J. D. Turner, "Dynamics of Criminal Law Administration in a Biracial Community of the Deep South," unpublished doctoral dissertation, Indiana University, Bloomington, 1956.

17. Edward Green, "Inter- and Intra-racial Crime Relative to Sentencing," *Journal of Criminal Law, Criminology and Police Science,* vol. 55, pp. 348–358, September, 1954.

18. S. S. Ulmer, "Supreme Court Behavior in Racial Exclusion Cases, 1935–1960," *The American Political Science Review,* vol. 56, pp. 325–330, June, 1963.

19. Felix Frankfurter, *The Case of Sacco and Vanzetti,* Academic Reprints, Stanford, Calif., 1954, pp. 11–12, 13–14.

20. Fred J. Strodtbeck, Rita M. James, and Charles Hawkins, "Social Status in Jury Deliberations," *American Sociological Review,* vol. 22, pp. 713–719, December, 1957.

21. *Report of the Attorney General's Committee on Poverty and the Administration of Criminal Justice: Poverty and the Administration of Federal Criminal Justice,* submitted to the Honorable Robert F. Kennedy, Attorney General of the United States, February 25, 1963.

22. An interesting colloquy between two professors of law with diametrically opposite views on this issue may be found in: Fred E. Imbau, "Public Safety v. Individual Civil Liberties: The Prosecutor's Stand," *Journal of Criminal Law, Criminology and Police Science,* vol. 53, pp. 85–89, March, 1962; Yale Kamisar, "Public Safety v. Individual Liberties: Some 'Facts' and 'Theories,'" *Journal of Criminal Law, Criminology and Police Science,* vol. 53, pp. 171–193, June, 1962; Fred E. Imbau, "More About Public Safety v. Individual Civil

Liberties," *Journal of Criminal Law, Criminology and Police Science,* vol. 53, pp. 329–332, September, 1962; Yale Kamisar, "Some Reflections on Criticizing the Courts and 'Policing the Police,'" *Journal of Criminal Law, Criminology and Police Science,* vol. 53, pp. 453–462, December, 1962.

Chapter Seven: Prevention, Imprisonment, Annihilation

1. Edwin Powers and Helen Witmer, *An Experiment in the Prevention of Delinquency: The Cambridge-Somerville Youth Study,* Columbia University Press, New York, 1951.
2. Gresham M. Sykes, *The Society of Captives,* Princeton University Press, Princeton, N.J., 1958.
3. Charles Spear, *Essays on the Punishment of Death,* published by the author, Boston, 1845, pp. 159–161.
4. Leon Radzinowicz, *A History of English Criminal Law, Vol. I, The Movement for Reform, 1750–1833,* The Macmillan Company, New York, 1948.
5. The most recent compilation of capital crimes and punishments in the United States, with only several slight errors, is to be found in Hugo A. Bedau, *The Death Penalty in America,* chap. 2, "The Law: The Crimes and the Offenses Punishable by Death," Doubleday & Company, Inc., Garden City, N.Y., 1964, pp. 39–52.
6. U.S. Department of Justice, Bureau of Prisons, *Executions, 1930–1963,* National Prisoner Statistics, no. 34., May, 1964.
7. George Ryley Scott, *The History of Capital Punishment,* Torchstream Books, London, 1950, pp. 186–187.
8. *Ibid.,* pp. 155–157.
9. Several reports of various errors of justice involving the execution of innocent, or presumably innocent men are to be found in: Scott, *op. cit.,* chap. XVIII, pp. 248–263; Frank Hartung, *On Capital Punishment,* Wayne State University, Detroit, Mich., Department of Sociology, 1952 (mimeo), pp. 29–33; R. T. Paget and Sydney Silverman, *Hanged and Innocent,* Victor Gollancz, Ltd., London, 1953; Leslie Hale, *Hanged in Error,* Penguin Books, Inc., Baltimore, 1961; Bedau, *op. cit.,* "Murder, Errors of Justice and Capital Punishment," pp. 434–452; Otto Pollak, "The Errors of Justice," *The Annals of the American Academy of Political and Social Science,* vol. 284, pp. 115–123, November, 1952.
10. Robert Dann, "The Deterrent Effect of Capital Punishment," Friends Social Service Series, Committee on Philanthropic Labor and Philadelphia Yearly Meeting of Friends, Bulletin 29, March, 1935.

11. Leonard D. Savitz, "A Study in Capital Punishment," *Journal of Criminal Law, Criminology and Police Science,* vol. 49, pp. 338–341, December, 1958.
12. William F. Graves, "A Doctor Looks at Capital Punishment," *Medical Arts and Sciences,* pp. 137–141, Fourth Quarter, 1956.
13. Thorsten Sellin, *The Death Penalty,* The American Law Institute, Philadelphia, 1959, pp. 23–34.
14. *Ibid.,* pp. 34–38.
15. *Minutes of Evidence Taken Before the Royal Commission on Capital Punishment,* Thirtieth Day, Witness: Professor Thorsten Sellin, His Majesty's Stationery Office, London, 1951.